Contents

Cover: One of the banners which flew over the General Post Office in Dublin during the Easter Rising of 1916
Front endpaper: British sentries on the roof of the Four Courts in Dublin in 1920
Back endpaper: Devastation in O'Connell Street after the Easter Rising

First published in 1969 by
Macdonald & Co (Publishers) Ltd
St Giles House 49 Poland St London W1
in the British Commonwealth and
American Heritage Press
551 Fifth Avenue New York NY 10017
in the United States of America
Library of Congress Catalogue
Card Number: 73-83794

Made and printed in Great Britain by
Purnell & Sons Ltd Paulton Somerset

OUT OF THE LION'S PAW

Ireland wins Her Freedom

Constantine FitzGibbon

For my Irish daughter Oonagh

David said moreover, The Lord that delivered me out of the paw of the lion, and out of the paw of the bear, he will deliver me out of the hand of this Philistine. . . . And he took his staff in his hand, and chose him five smooth stones out of the brook, and put them in a shepherd's bag which he had, even in a scrip; and his sling was in his hand; and he drew near to the Philistine.
1 Samuel 17, vv. 37 & 40

Visual material collected by George Morrison

Macdonald Library of the 20th Century
General Editor: John Roberts

DUBLIN TRAMWAYS COMPANY

Chapter 1

A sombre legacy

Ireland's struggle for freedom centres on two main events: the Easter Rising in 1916, which united most of the country in active opposition to the British, and the Revolution of 1919 which ended with the establishment of the Irish Republic. But the circumstances that led to these are of an intense complexity: historical, social, political, and perhaps above all psychological.

The psychological complexity, from the English point of view, can be traced to a general misunderstanding of the Irish character and of Irish desires. The Irish view of the world is as different from that of the English, indeed perhaps more different, than that of the Germans or even of the French. The English were bewildered by the fact that, as the Gaelic-speaking population shrank, most Irishmen, and all educated Irishmen, spoke English and wrote it as well as, and often better than, most Englishmen. They were further bewildered by the fact that a very large proportion of the Irish governing class was of English, or Anglo-Norman, ancestry. The English had not grasped the fact that in the two centuries which preceded the Easter Rising – the centuries since the passing of the Penal Laws against Irish Roman Catholics, the brutal smashing of what was left of the old Irish aristocracy, and the wholesale theft of Irish land – it was precisely these Protestant gentlemen, Grattan, Tone, Parnell, and so on, who had led the Irish in their longing to be free of alien rule. Were they not traitors thus to align themselves with the 'mere Irish' who were, by legal and religious definition and economic subjugation, reduced to the status of second-class citizens in their own country? At least Washington, Jefferson, and Franklin had never sided with the Redskins against the Redcoats.

The reason for this gross misunderstanding was that the English in England did not realise that the Irish way of life in Ireland was in many ways – at least in terms of human relationships – culturally superior to the English way, less brutal, less materialistic, more spiritual, more dignified, with infinitely less snobbery and class distinc-

Left: *The port of Dublin in the 1860s with the Customs House* tion, directed more towards human happiness than to the acquisition of wealth or objects. Always technologically backward and politically centrifugal, the Irish were overwhelmed throughout a thousand and more years by waves of conquerors, and from 1170 they all came from England or Scotland. If those conquerors remained in Ireland they became, as the English would and did say, seduced by the ease and pleasure of an Irish attitude that looks towards charm and gaiety, wit and piety, rather than towards profit: they became 'more Irish than the Irish'.

Only in parts of Ulster did the policy of plantation—that is to say the importation of an alien population—prove permanently 'successful'. There the native Irish were expelled in the early 17th century and the settlers were able to create a homogeneous society, based on strong religious beliefs of their own. The other plantations, both before and later, in the rest of Ireland soon decayed into mere class distinction, fanned periodically into extreme mutual hostility. Ulster apart, Ireland remained an occupied rather than assimilated territory. The awareness of nationhood was never lost by the Irish, and the demarcation between the conquerors and conquered of past generations became very blurred. After the Act of Union of 1800 Ireland's own parliament was dissolved, and the country was in essence governed from London, by Englishmen, rather than by its own Protestant governing class of English origin.

The English had much to offer—administrative and commercial skills, agricultural expertise, the Protestant religion. Few of the Irish were interested in these gifts. And this the English, in England, dismissed as feckless ingratitude. That the Irish had different values from their own was regarded as funny—and the 'stage Irishman' was created in London, the equivalent of the comical 'darkie' on the stages of old New York. The fact that English might had always, eventually, crushed Irish rebellion was remembered: the fact that Irishmen had fought with immense distinction in all the major armies of Europe, not least in that of Great Britain, was often forgotten. From the point of view of the English governing class throughout most of the 19th century and up to the First World War, 'Paddy-and-his-pig' was essentially a comical, childlike figure. He should know, in English terms, his proper station in life. Perhaps, at a pinch, the Anglo-Irish (an odious, almost meaningless term) might run this province of Great Britain: but Paddy, never.

On the other hand these Irishmen were politically troublesome and, furthermore, the English of the late Vic-

__Right:__ Punchestown races, the sport of all the people, where class, race, and religion were temporarily forgotten in the 1860s

torian age were a decent lot on the whole, in their stern, paternalistic way. By the latter part of the 19th century, the great Liberal leader W.E.Gladstone had become convinced that the Irish should be given partial sovereignty over their own affairs—the process which was to be known as Home Rule. Gladstone introduced the first Home Rule Bill in the British House of Commons in 1886. An Irish parliament was to be set up, with responsibility for local affairs, while Westminster was to retain authority over military, naval, and foreign affairs. The King of England would remain King of Ireland.

Charles Stewart Parnell, the leader of the 86 Irish MPs, who supported Home Rule—Ireland sent 103 to Westminster at this time—backed Gladstone's Liberals in support of this bill but a sufficient number of Liberals defected (they called themselves Liberal Unionists) to defeat the bill and bring about the fall of the government. This was to be the fate of a similar Home Rule Bill in 1893 which passed through the House of Commons only to be thrown out in the House of Lords, which at that time could reject all legislation except money bills. A third was passed at last in 1913, by which time the power of the Lords had been cut down by the Parliament Act of 1911 so that they could only postpone its enactment for two years. With the outbreak of the First World War Asquith's Liberal government decided that the act, which had received the royal assent, should not be implemented until that war was over.

Irish nationalism in modern times has always tended to have two wings, the constitutional and the revolutionary. These have sometimes alternated, sometimes coexisted. When Grattan's parliament was in decline, the Rebellion of 1798 dealt it its death blow, and for a while revolutionaries such as the United Irishmen, Tone, and Emmet became the leaders of a lost cause. Daniel O'Connell achieved much for his compatriots by constitutional means, in particular the Catholic Emancipation Act of 1829—which gave the Roman Catholic civil rights—but he could not get a bill to repeal the Act of Union through the House of Commons, and any hope that his methods might bring about a political solution with Britain was blasted by the horrors of the 1846 Famine and the massive emigration that ensued. (Over 8,000,000 in 1841, the population fell by 2,000,000 within the next ten years: in 1881 it was about 5,000,000: in the 1964 census it was a little over 4,000,000 including both the Republic and Northern Ireland.) The pendulum swung again. The Young Ireland movement of 1848 was akin to the great liberal-revolutionary movement that swept all Europe in that year. It

Left: *The dire poverty of Dublin in the 1880s, a slum street*

was crushed, and most of its leaders who did not flee to the United States were deported to Australia. The movement was destroyed but its spirit lingered on in the Irish Republican Brotherhood, founded in 1858.

The IRB (which must not be confused with the IRA or Irish Republican Army of much later date) was a secret society. It probably never numbered more than 2,000 including those members of the Brotherhood who lived in America, Australia, England, and elsewhere. The majority of its members were what might loosely be called 'intellectuals' and in this, in their determination, and in their secrecy they bore a certain resemblance to their contemporaries, the secret Russian revolutionary groups culminating in Lenin's small Bolshevik Party. Unlike the Bolsheviks, however, their aims were political rather than economic. They were patriots, dedicated to the ideal of national independence, and were prepared to use all means – including force – to achieve this end. They infiltrated all the patriotic movements, even such apparently non-political bodies as the Gaelic Athletic Association, which promoted the playing of Irish games, and the Gaelic League, primarily concerned with the preservation of the Irish language. Many movements they controlled. They provided, as it were, the general staff of what was to become a mass movement for Irish freedom from British rule. Their fortnightly publication, *Irish Freedom,* founded in 1910, advocated complete republican government for the whole of Ireland. It is significant that all the men who signed the proclamation of an Irish Republic on Easter Monday, 1916, were members of the IRB.

The Fenians, the secret society which had attempted a revolution by violence that failed in 1867, were led by the IRB and indeed might be described as its activist wing. They were the direct political descendants of the Young Ireland movement and the direct ancestors of the men of 1916. On the other hand the terrorists who murdered Lord Frederick Cavendish, Chief Secretary for Ireland, and the Under-Secretary, Thomas Burke, in Phoenix Park in 1882 were not Fenians, though so described in the British press, but members of another secret society. It would seem improbable that the IRB had encouraged this act of terrorism which outraged public opinion and made Parnell's task to secure Home Rule even more difficult than it already was.

For there was much violence in Ireland in the second half of the 19th century, and by no means all of it was political. For generations violence had been endemic in the countryside. The Irish tenant farmers and farm

Right: *Gladstone discomfited over Irish Home Rule.* ***Far right:*** *Parnell* ***(top),*** *Kitty O'Shea* ***(centre),*** *Gladstone* ***(bottom)***

labourers believed, usually correctly, that the land which they worked had been stolen from their ancestors by their landlords' ancestors. Absentee landlords – many of whom spent all their time in England, often sitting in the Lords and thus totally opposed to any freedom for Ireland – sub-contracted to agents, often very hard men whose sole interest was to extract maximum rents. The position of the tenant farmer was such that any improvement he made to his farm could, and not infrequently did, result in increased rent. Such farms decayed. Agricultural misery was increased by a badly-drafted Land Act of 1870, worsened by a disastrous agricultural slump that followed throughout the decade. Tillage became profitless, and pasture the main form of farming. This meant less work on the land, and even though the young emigrated in huge numbers, the standard of living of those who remained continued to decline. Villages became rural slums and many 'farms' were mere hovels. Only with the passage of a new Land Act in 1881 did the position of the small tenant farmer begin to improve. He was now given the three Fs; fair rent, freedom to sell his right of occupancy to the highest bidder, and fixture of tenancy.

For the countryside had been further embittered by evictions. Despite the rapid shrinkage of the population, many landlords found that they still had too many tenants when they switched from corn to cattle and fewer hands were needed. More grazing land was wanted and from the landlords' point of view these little farms, or 'cabins' as they were called, were in the way. It was logical, *laissez-faire* economics in Ireland in the 1860s, as it was logical, Marxist economics in Russia in the 1930s, to evict these redundant peasants, particularly since many lived by subsistence farming of tiny plots and could pay no cash rents. This caused immense bitterness. So too had the collection of tithes in one form or another from Roman Catholics to support the established Protestant Church of Ireland, before the Church of Ireland was disestablished and most of its lands sold. There were many murders in the countryside.

And in Dublin, once a great and beautiful capital, urban misery increased, crime and prostitution were commonplace – as indeed they were in London – and large parts of the fair city degenerated into slum. Only in one part of the country, the largely Protestant north-east, did industrialisation begin to improve the lot of the inhabitants. Belfast became a comparatively flourishing, though ugly and brutal, city.

The nadir was, perhaps, 1867, the year of the Fenian Rising. In 1869 the Church of Ireland was **17**▷

Left: *Cardinal Wiseman's lambs: the English fear of Popery*

Fuel-for the fire to come

Evictions were the cruellest economic misery of the Irish 19th century. In an attempt to improve the income they derived from land, many landowners evicted unprofitable tenant-farmers and put the land down for grazing. For most of the century the tenant-farmers had no legal right of tenure. When they refused to leave their wretched homes, the landlords could have them forcibly evicted **(right)** by the constabulary and even by the military. As the picture below shows, the evicted would sometimes squat in turf-built hovels rather than move away. To the Irish tenantry this policy seemed a continuation in a new form of the centuries-old English spoliation of Ireland by the theft and confiscation of Irish land in the interests of the alien conqueror. One direct consequence of the policy pursued by the landlords was the Land War, when the tenants retaliated by a mass refusal to pay rent: landlords and agents were attacked and not infrequently murdered.

disestablished. In 1870 Isaac Butt founded the Home Rule League, which gave the nucleus of a policy to Roman Catholics and Protestants alike, who were horrified by the decay of their country and wanted to increase its independence from Westminster. Michael Davitt, a Fenian imprisoned from 1871 to 1878, founded the Land League as soon as he was released. His whole life, both before and after prison, was devoted to transforming the chaotic misery and violence of the countrymen into a political force. And, more important still, Parnell became the effective leader of the Irish Party in 1877, at the age of thirty-one. He immediately set about fusing the agrarian and the political interests of his compatriots into one united, constitutionalist front. Never an advocate of revolution, for thirteen years this handsome young Protestant was 'the uncrowned King of Ireland', of all Ireland except the Unionist landowners and their supporters, principally the Protestants of the north-east. During this period much was achieved. Gladstone's Land Act of 1881 had gone some way to redressing the wrongs of the tenant farmers. This process was more or less completed by the Land Act of 1903 whereby the tenant farmers received government loans on easy and long terms to buy their farms. The defeated Home Rule Bill of 1886, though accompanied by anti-Catholic rioting in Belfast – an ominous warning of things to come – showed at least that Ireland's wrongs were accepted by England's leading statesman and his party and thus gave a promise of partial liberty in the future. For the time being the IRB was prepared to accept such constitutional methods, though should these fail the alternative method was never ruled out.

When Parnell was cited as co-respondent in a divorce action by Kitty O'Shea's husband in 1890, his party split and so, too, did the country. Irish Roman Catholicism was then even more puritanical than it is to-day. The hierarchy spoke, and the priests preached, against the Protestant adulterer. The British nonconformists, a powerful force within the Liberal Party, took the same view. Gladstone could hardly have come to his defence, even had he so wished. The Unionists exploited the scandal to the full. And Parnell was dropped. He married his beloved, but the next year he died aged forty-five.

With him, and with the defeat of the Second Home Rule Bill in 1893, Irish unity behind the constitutional wing of the Irish freedom movement was also dead. It was to be reborn, but now behind the revolutionary wing, a quarter of a century later.

Left: *Further scenes during* ***(top)*** *and after eviction* ***(bottom)***

106

Chapter 2

The Golden Sunset

During the first decade of the 20th century Ireland was, on the whole, happier, more prosperous, and more pacified than for a hundred years and more. The Land Act of 1903, sponsored by George Wyndham and backed by Sir Anthony MacDonnell, and soon amended in further favour of the Irish small farmers, removed one of the major economic grievances. Irish troops had fought bravely in the Boer War, so bravely that Edward VII created a new regiment of foot guards, the Irish Guards. Irish nationalists had not attempted to exploit England's initial difficulties in this war in the Irish interest. Home Rule was, it seemed, inevitable before too long. In 1900 John Redmond, a Parnellite, was elected leader of the Irish Nationalist Party and set about repairing the rifts within his party against the day when the Liberals should return to office – which they did in 1906 – and a new Home Rule Bill might be expected. He reunited his party and became indeed a respected Westminster politician, though in Ireland itself he never achieved the stature that makes a great national leader. Indeed, it was later said in Ireland that he spent too much time in London and that he was gradually losing touch with his own country.

In all save the most bigoted Protestant areas of the north-east, most Irishmen of all religious denominations were becoming more and more reconciled to the idea of partial self-government in a country that was quiet, law-abiding, and comparatively well-off, compared to the past that is, for there was still great poverty both in the country and the cities. Emigration declined slightly, and was to decline more rapidly with the agricultural prosperity created by the First World War. Indeed, an English general was to declare, during the Anglo-Irish War, that this was the cause of the trouble: there were, he said, 100,000 more young men in Ireland than there should be. But that lay in the future. Now Dublin Castle, the seat of the Lord Lieutenant and also the centre of the British administration in Ireland, was a bogus palace in a sham

Left: *Sackville Street, now O'Connell Street, showing the General Post Office and O'Connell's statue. The date is about 1890*

capital. The tea parties and the croquet upon its lawns and those of the great landowners gave pleasure and still evoke a curious, faded, nostalgic charm. In its ballrooms young Irish ladies danced with young officers of the British army who had not yet heard of Mons or Ypres or Passchendaele. All those who could afford it went hunting, or so it seems, while even those who could not went racing. In the country it was the period when the Ascendancy (the term used for the Protestant Anglo-Irish aristocracy) regarded 'the mere Irish' with more affection, humour, and far greater tolerance than they had ever shown before. And the 'dear, dirty Dublin' of the period was to be preserved forever in the amber of Ireland's greatest novel, James Joyce's *Ulysses,* though this was not published until 1920.

Just as the *belle époque* and the Edwardian interlude in England have appeared in the eyes of posterity as a golden sunset before the bloody blackness so soon to come, so this period of Ireland's history has a flavour that lingers and enchants. It was the period of Ireland's great renaissance – or so it then seemed – the period of Lady Gregory, the Abbey Theatre, Yeats, Moore, Synge, Joyce, Shaw, AE, and intensive Celtic scholarship. Happiness seemed at last to be taking root in Irish soil. Had there been no First World War, perhaps happiness might have done so. But perhaps not. In the 20th century, economic progress and even social and cultural well-being have by no means invariably produced political contentment, whether in Ireland or elsewhere.

And English rule was still based upon the threat of force, and Irish resistance to that rule was still prepared to use force in the last resort. Urban economic issues, additional to but different from the old and partially resolved agricultural ones, were slowly coming into prominence as a more prosperous Ireland became slightly more industrialised: the class war, in fact, was adding another dimension, though only marginally, to the Irish scene. In the west the sky might be golden: in the east black war clouds were piling into the sky. As the years went by, the possibility, then the probability, of war with Germany must have been discussed by the young Irish ladies and the doomed British officers between waltzes and polkas and the new-fangled foxtrots. It was discussed elsewhere in Ireland, and also among those members of the IRB who lived in England, America, or Australia. If Home Rule were to be delayed much longer, this would surely be the opportunity to attempt, once again, the other solution?

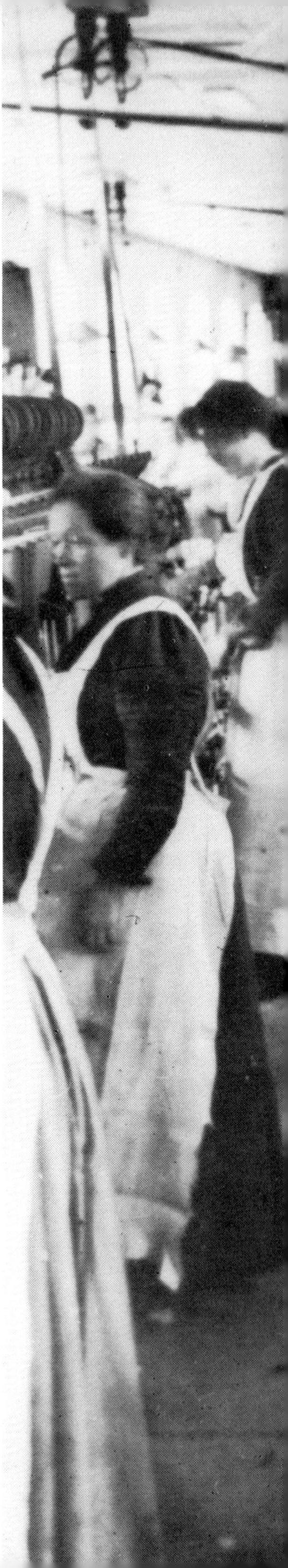

***Right:** A Belfast linen mill in the 1880s. Belfast had already become a growing industrial city, prosperous but ugly and brutal*

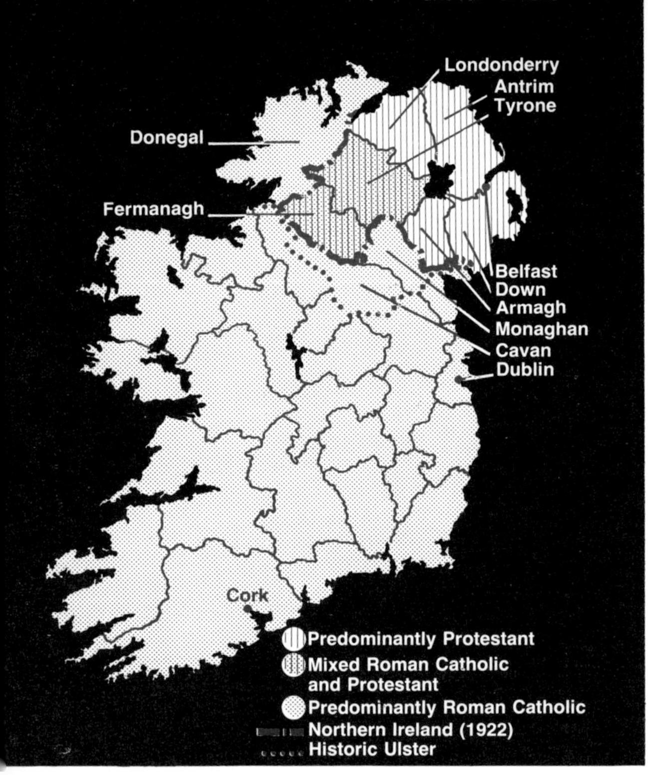
Londonderry
Antrim
Tyrone
Donegal
Fermanagh
Belfast
Down
Armagh
Monaghan
Cavan
Dublin
Cork
Predominantly Protestant
Mixed Roman Catholic and Protestant
Predominantly Roman Catholic
Northern Ireland (1922)
Historic Ulster

English rule was based, in the countryside, on the Royal Irish Constabulary, an armed, paramilitary police force, living largely in barracks and some 10,000 strong. The men of the RIC were almost all Irishmen, knew their districts thoroughly and at least until 1916 were, with a very few exceptions, entirely loyal to the Crown. They were well-trained, well if simply equipped, and only moderately unpopular. They were as competent as were their cousins, doing a similar job in Boston and New York. Dublin Castle could rely on the RIC not only to put down any local disturbance but also to supply regular and reliable intelligence concerning conditions throughout the country.

In Dublin the police were not normally armed, though of course there were weapons available. They were about 1,000 men, organised on the model of the London police. The Special Branch was concerned with politics. These plain-clothes detectives were supposed to infiltrate nationalist, republican, and left-wing organisations and inform the Castle what, if anything, was afoot. The Specials, however, do not appear to have been particularly good at this job and certainly do not seem to have infiltrated the IRB successfully.

Behind these police forces stood the British army and navy. In the front line there were the British regiments stationed in Ireland and also Naval Intelligence which had the task of infiltrating Irish patriotic associations abroad and of preventing or intercepting contacts between Irish extremists and Great Britain's other potential enemies in Germany and elsewhere. In the second line stood the British army in Great Britain, which could speedily reinforce the troops in Ireland, and the Royal Navy which could easily blockade the Irish coast.

Such was the apparatus of occupation and exploitation. (Exploitation is not an exaggeration. A government committee, presided over by Sir Henry Primrose in 1912, reported that Sir Anthony MacDonnell, who had been Under-Secretary for Ireland from 1902 to 1908, estimated the treasure extracted from Ireland by the British government, and used elsewhere since the Act of Union of 1800, at £350,000,000 [approximately $1,680,000,000 at the contemporary rate of exchange]. This confirmed a government report of 1896, that Ireland had been severely over-taxed ever since the Act of Union as compared to the remainder of the United Kingdom. Far vaster sums

Top left: *A map showing the religious demography of Ireland at the time of the treaty partitioning the country.* ***Bottom left:*** *The throne room in Dublin Castle, an example of the attempt at display which failed to conceal the essential tawdriness of the viceregal court.* ***Left:*** *Dublin Castle, the hub of British power* had been taken out by private enterprise.) This apparatus enjoyed the active support of the Irish and English Unionists; the rest of the British population, with only a few exceptions, gave it passive support; Redmond's party and the great majority of the Irish were only passively opposed to British rule in those days, and the prospect of Home Rule increased their tolerance; its only real enemies at the beginning of the century were the IRB, to whom were soon to be added the new movement called *Sinn Fein* and, primarily for economic reasons, the socialists and important parts of the trade unions.

An influx of new blood

Waiting for Home Rule, however, the old IRB had, by the century's first decade, become almost moribund as young Fenians turned into old dreamers. There were exceptions among them, of whom Thomas Clarke, born in 1858, was perhaps to achieve the greatest fame. But as the decade wore on, younger and more active men joined the Brotherhood, particularly in Ulster where tension was rising but also in the south. Sean MacDermott and Bulmer Hobson founded *Irish Freedom* in 1910 and among the contributors was yet another young member of the IRB, a schoolmaster by the name of Padraic Pearse. These and other young men blew the dying embers of Fenianism into flame once again. Not only were all the signatories to the declaration of the Irish Republic members of the IRB, but so too were most of the Irish leaders in the Anglo-Irish war that followed.

Sinn Fein was not originally a republican movement. Created by a journalist of great talent, Arthur Griffith, it was a constitutional but anti-parliamentarian movement which later became a political party—it contested and lost its first by-election in 1908—and later still its name and its organisation were to become the fulcrum of the whole revolutionary movement, only to disintegrate and disappear with even greater speed in the brief period between the end of the Anglo-Irish War and the outbreak of the Irish Civil War.

Sinn Fein is usually translated as 'ourselves alone', and this is perhaps the best rendition in English of a complicated Irish concept. It means, first of all and above all, independence from British rule. But since Irish history has cast so long a shadow across Irish politics, it had a secondary meaning. For many centuries the Irish had hoped for the help of England's enemies to get rid of English rule. The Spaniards and the French had let them down as the Germans were to do in 1916. This was less for any lack of eagerness on the part of England's enemies to defeat Britain in Ireland than because of geographical-military complications (tides, prevailing winds, and so on,

not to mention the Royal Navy's habitual control of the seas around Ireland). Thus *Sinn Fein* also meant that the Irish must rely on themselves alone to rid themselves of their English rulers. For the English, in the years to come, the 'Shinners' were to be the epitome of violent republicanism in Ireland. In fact the party, which only had its first annual convention as late as 1905, was essentially democratic, and Arthur Griffith was not a republican at all. His articles in the paper he edited were never fanatical, though always patriotic. This is one reason why he could and did attract more and more of the younger and more ardent members away from Redmond's rather staid Nationalist Party.

In the beginning he advocated a Dual Monarchy on the Austro-Hungarian model. He was opposed to the Home Rulers on tactical rather than strategic grounds. He wished the Irish MPs to boycott the Westminster parliament and to meet separately, as an Irish parliament or Dail; he wished to see Irish appeal courts set up in opposition to the British law courts, and for these latter to be boycotted by the Irish people; he wanted an Irish stock exchange and an Irish bank; and, in the coming war, he hoped that Ireland might be helped by England's enemies to set up an Irish government, but he knew that this was only possible if a *de facto* government, in skeleton form at least, was already prepared to take over and become the *de jure* government of his country. All these ideas he presented in his newspaper, *The United Irishman*. Most of them were turned into reality in the struggle to come.

Though more radical in his nationalism than Redmond, and less so than the young men of *Irish Freedom,* in social and economic matters Griffith was not radical at all. His paper bore the same name as that of the Young Ireland movement, and, like the men of 1848, it was a bourgeois revolution using proletarian forces that he desired and which, perhaps more than most, he eventually brought about. He had no wish to see the class structure overturned nor the economy remodelled: he merely wanted the British government in Ireland replaced, *in toto,* by an Irish government, beneath the Crown.

Since the IRB was also essentially uninterested in economic and social, as opposed to political, revolution, the events to come would not produce a new post-capitalist society: they would merely modify the old capitalist society very slightly and substitute Irishmen for Englishmen in the seats of power.

The fact that Ireland was an almost entirely agrarian society is as irrelevant to the nature of the Irish revolu-

Left: *A Dublin street scene about 1907, the period which was immortalised by James Joyce in his famous novel 'Ulysses'* tion as is the fact that the Irish are a profoundly religious people. In 1917 the Russians were both, in at least equal measure. The basic difference is that the Irish, for their good fortune or not according to taste, lacked a Lenin. And while the IRB bore in many technical, above all conspiratorial, respects a strong resemblance to Lenin's pre-1917 Bolsheviks, it was far more broadly based, in that it saw itself representing the whole Irish nation, and had a far more concrete objective, the overthrow of English rule. Even the extreme left wing among the republicans were concerned with the expropriation of the *foreign* expropriators and not with the liquidation of an Irish governing and property-owning class, which indeed scarcely existed and which most of the republicans were anxious to create. Thus from Lenin's point of view it must have seemed an old-fashioned, nationalist revolution: from the point of view of the leaders in the other British colonies who were to get rid of British rule after the Second World War it must have appeared ultra-modern. Certainly many of them used it, consciously or not, as the model for their own revolutions.

This does not mean that the IRB's leaders were necessarily out of sympathy with militant socialism. Some were and some were not. Irish socialism was directed against a capitalist apparatus that had its roots, heart, and pulmonary apparatus in London. Its militancy was therefore directed against British power in Ireland and, as such, acceptable. Furthermore the nature of Irish socialism changed when James Connolly took over the leadership from Jim Larkin in 1913. There had been a bloodstained strike and lock-out of the ITGWU (Irish Transport and General Workers' Union), producing much misery, violence, and looting shortly before Larkin's departure for America. Larkin was a most passionate and extremist orator who would have felt more at home in the Paris Commune than in the respectable offices of a modern socialist party. Connolly was a far more modern type of socialist, indeed in many ways an innovator. In an age when socialism, in theory at least, was an international creed, Connolly deliberately attempted, and in large measure succeeded, in creating a synthesis of socialism and nationalism. He wished to harness both these forces to found an Irish Socialist Republic. But if his socialists were increasingly nationalists too, and if

Right: *The Green room of the Abbey Theatre about 1905 with Lennox Robinson the playwright on the left.* ***Bottom right:*** *The original programme of the Abbey Theatre. The first decade of the 20th century saw a great period in Irish culture particularly in literature and the theatre—men such as Yeats, Moore, Joyce* ***(top right),*** *and Shaw earned international reputations*

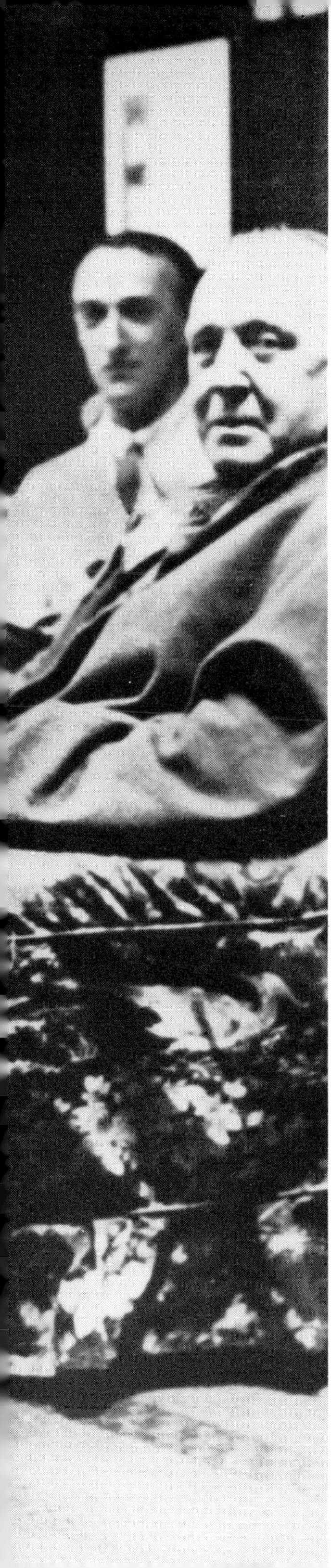

his synthesis was also and in large measure accepted by the intellectuals of the age, he won few converts either among the agricultural majority or among the nationalist middle class. Furthermore he did not produce a fully logical synthesis of his Marxism and his nationalism. Nor did he organise a party which could throw up another leader after his death in 1916. Had he lived, it is possible that the Irish Labour Party would have had a great and constructive role to play in the years to come. But he died.

In order to ensure that his men should not again be defenceless against strike-breakers he organised the Citizen Army during the winter of 1913-14. It was led and trained by Captain Jack White, a former member of the British armed forces whose father is said to have been a British general. This small force was tough and efficient. It received the full support of the IRB and fought with great courage and skill during Easter Week 1916.

A friend of Connolly's was Constance, Countess Markievicz, a well-born Irishwoman who had moved from the boredom—for women such as she—of Dublin Castle society to the dangers of militant socialism and republicanism. She was concerned with the republicans' female auxiliaries, which became the League of Women or *Cumann na mBan,* and also organised a sort of republican boys' brigade, the *Fianna na hEireann,* trained to act as runners, signallers, and so on. Both of these organisations were to be of great importance in the struggles ahead.

Thus were the two major power blocs aligned for the struggle to come. In 1910 few, if any, knew that it would be coming so soon. The eyes of the Irish people and of the English people too were fixed on Westminster where Asquith's Liberal government had to rely on Redmond's Irish Party to survive while Redmond was insistent that a Home Rule Bill be forced through a still recalcitrant House of Lords. In the north-east the Unionists were beginning to threaten and to speak again of resistance to Home Rule. And in Berlin, St. Petersburg, Vienna, and Paris men in well-cut suits and elegant uniforms must occasionally have considered Ireland when wondering what their equivalents in London, in better-cut suits and almost equally elegant uniforms, would decide on The Day. After March 1914, it may safely be assumed that the references to Ireland in the minutes of Europe's chancelleries became considerably longer and more detailed.

Left: *The reality of power, British troops in Limerick, about 1900*

OI-1556
OI-2556
OI-497
OI-2615
BO1076
OI-282

Chapter 3

'Ulster will fight'

In 1910 two general elections were held in the United Kingdom. After the first of these, the Liberals and Unionists so balanced one another that Asquith would need Labour and Irish support to carry the reforms his party wanted, the most important of which was a drastic limitation in the powers of the House of Lords. But success in that was essential to the passing of Home Rule, to which Liberals were again turning. So the Irish were as tied to them as they were to the Irish. Asquith sent up a Bill limiting the power of the Lords, and the Lords hesitated. A second election was held.

Throughout 1910 Home Rule was coming into the forefront of the nations' political consciousness, of the English nation's as of the Irish. And lines began to harden. The second election left Asquith where he was, but gave Redmond two more seats. After it the Liberal Party, with its Labour Party supporters, held 314 seats, the Conservative Unionists 272, and the Irish Nationalist Party 84. The Irish MPs were almost sure to vote with the Liberals; nevertheless, if Asquith were to renege his promise of Home Rule, they could immediately defeat the rest of his programme and, indeed, turn the government out. Home Rule was just around the corner. In August 1911 the British Parliament Act became law. The House of Lords could now only postpone legislation that had passed through the House of Commons, for a maximum of about two years. It seemed that the Irish had won the game. Home Rule could be anticipated for 1913 or, at the latest, 1914. Various government committees, such as the Primrose Committee already mentioned, were set up to discuss its details, with this date in view. For a moment it seemed the age-old tragedy was ended, and without bloodshed.

The moment did not last for long. *Sinn Fein,* the IRB, and indeed the whole Irish nation with the exception of the Unionists accepted the prospect of almost immediate Home Rule with relief. But when, also in 1911, Redmond and his party voted with the government for a bill where-

Left: *Motorcycle brigade of the Ulster Volunteers parades, 1914*

THE ULSTER KING-AT-ARMS.
HOME RULE
NATIONALIST
VOLUNTEERS

Chapter 3
'Ulster will fight'

In 1910 two general elections were held in the United Kingdom. After the first of these, the Liberals and Unionists so balanced one another that Asquith would need Labour and Irish support to carry the reforms his party wanted, the most important of which was a drastic limitation in the powers of the House of Lords. But success in that was essential to the passing of Home Rule, to which Liberals were again turning. So the Irish were as tied to them as they were to the Irish. Asquith sent up a Bill limiting the power of the Lords, and the Lords hesitated. A second election was held.

Throughout 1910 Home Rule was coming into the forefront of the nations' political consciousness, of the English nation's as of the Irish. And lines began to harden. The second election left Asquith where he was, but gave Redmond two more seats. After it the Liberal Party, with its Labour Party supporters, held 314 seats, the Conservative Unionists 272, and the Irish Nationalist Party 84. The Irish MPs were almost sure to vote with the Liberals; nevertheless, if Asquith were to renege his promise of Home Rule, they could immediately defeat the rest of his programme and, indeed, turn the government out. Home Rule was just around the corner. In August 1911 the British Parliament Act became law. The House of Lords could now only postpone legislation that had passed through the House of Commons, for a maximum of about two years. It seemed that the Irish had won the game. Home Rule could be anticipated for 1913 or, at the latest, 1914. Various government committees, such as the Primrose Committee already mentioned, were set up to discuss its details, with this date in view. For a moment it seemed the age-old tragedy was ended, and without bloodshed.

The moment did not last for long. *Sinn Fein,* the IRB, and indeed the whole Irish nation with the exception of the Unionists accepted the prospect of almost immediate Home Rule with relief. But when, also in 1911, Redmond and his party voted with the government for a bill where-

Left: *Motorcycle brigade of the Ulster Volunteers parades, 1914* by MPs, including themselves, should be paid there was a spasm of revulsion among the purest Irish nationalists. It was, they felt, one thing for Ireland's elected representatives to use British parliamentary tactics in Ireland's interest: it was quite another for those representatives to accept, indeed vote for, payment of themselves by the Crown. This tactical error on Redmond's part—had he and his party abstained, the bill would still have gone through—cost him dear. In the short run it led to the immediate strengthening of *Sinn Fein* at the expense of the Nationalist Party: in the long run, which was to be a mere six years, it was probably the first step towards the total extinction of that party.

Even more ominous were the reactions to Home Rule from Belfast. In the nine countries that form the Province of Ulster there were, according to the 1911 census, some 700,000 Roman Catholics and some 900,000 Protestants of all persuasions. (Ulstermen then amounted to a little over one third of the whole population of Ireland.) In parts of Ulster, such as Belfast and the Counties Down and Antrim, the Protestants outnumbered the Roman Catholics by as much as two to one, though the distribution was not uniform. In others, such as Cavan, Monaghan, and Donegal, the ratio was reversed. In the remaining four counties there was a rough parity. Yet the extreme Unionists in Belfast now proclaimed that loyalist 'Protestant' Ulster was about to be sold into bondage to the disloyal 'Catholic' portion of the island. And the possibility of partition began to be mentioned both in Belfast and in London.

This injection of the religious issue into what had long ago become a purely political, and marginally economic, situation was curious and very dishonest. Only quite recently had the Presbyterians allied themselves with the Church of Ireland Unionists and the British Conservatives: in Ireland until about the time of the Famine they had been among the most vociferous republicans, while their co-religionaries in Scotland together with the other nonconformist sects in England and Wales continued to vote Liberal or Labour. Furthermore the Church of Rome, whatever the private sympathies of Irish priests may have been, had always taken meticulous care not to meddle in Anglo-Irish politics, save only to deplore and discourage all revolutionary activity of any sort. The hierarchy officially and publicly disapproved of the IRB as it had of the Fenians: only in the educational field did it become directly involved in politics. Certainly Irish republicanism, and even more so the Home Rule movement, had no religious basis whatsoever save in so far as Irish Catholicism was a vital strand in the Irish cultural fabric. Now religious fanaticism became the basis of

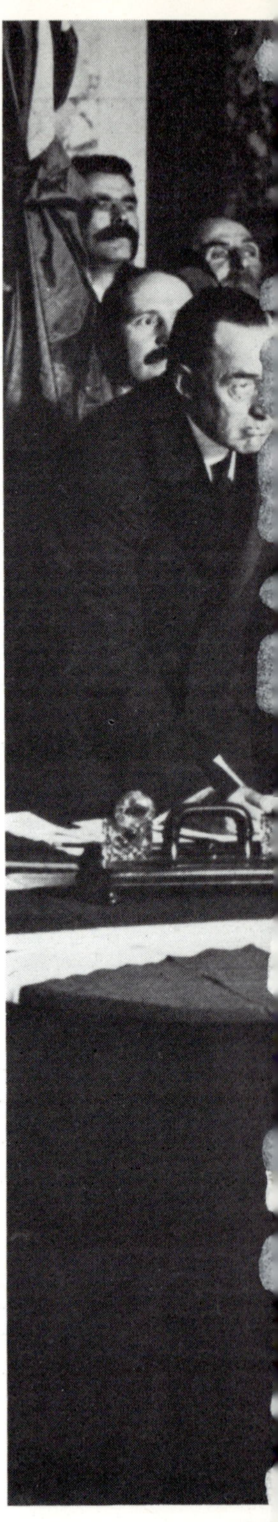

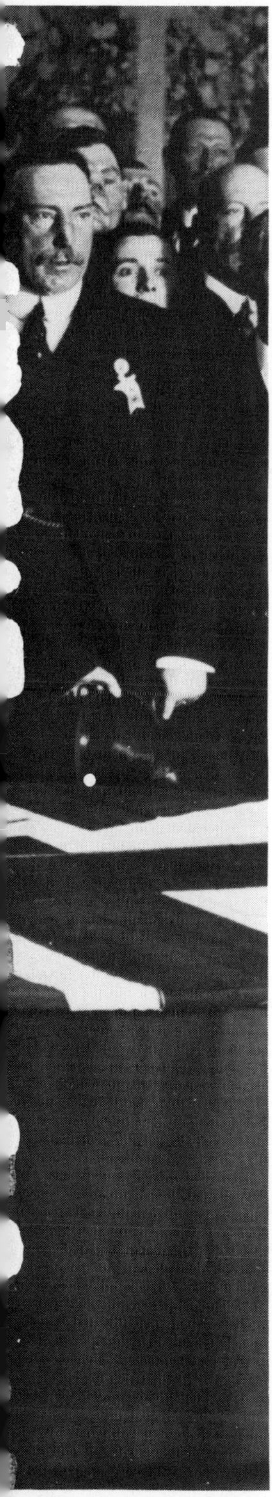

'Ulster' separatism from the still unborn and only partly autonomous Irish state. The slogan 'Home Rule Means Rome Rule' was a deliberate appeal to the historical, latent anti-Catholicism of the English people as a whole and of the English ruling class in particular.

Sir Edward Carson, the Dublin barrister whose skill had sent Oscar Wilde to prison, was one of the Unionist MPs representing Trinity College, had been Solicitor General in the last Conservative government and was a member of the Privy Council. He now became a leader of what, for purposes of abbreviation, must be called the Ulstermen, ably supported by F. E. Smith, later Lord Birkenhead, Walter Long, and other political and social luminaries. Carson functioned primarily in London and was indefatigable in his attempts to prevent Home Rule. The leader in Belfast was James Craig, later Lord Craigavon. Carson's main interest was to preserve the Union. For this purpose he was prepared to use Ulster intransigence. Craig thought rather as an Ulsterman, determined that his province be not ruled by Roman Catholics in Dublin. Behind both stood Bonar Law, a future Conservative leader and prime minister, a Canadian-born Ulsterman.

The violence begins

Craig called a mass meeting of anti-Home Rule Ulstermen as early as 23rd September 1911. The attendance was estimated at 100,000, and violent speeches were made. Two days later the Ulster Unionist Council began to prepare an Ulster provisional government. In the following year preparation went ahead for the creation of an Ulster Volunteer Force, a military organization. Also in 1912 the Protestant Belfast mob, encouraged by these leaders, initiated what can only be called a pogrom directed against their Roman Catholic fellow-citizens. The express purpose of this pogrom, which was to last for many years, was to drive the Catholics from their homes. Immediately at the great Belfast shipyards some two thousand Roman Catholic workers were physically expelled from their jobs by their work-mates. All this received the explicit approval of the Conservative Party leaders in London and of the Unionist leaders in Belfast, while Liberal leaders, such as Winston Churchill, were treated with contempt and abuse when they tried to justify Home Rule before Ulster audiences. (In the years to come the Belfast pogrom was to be hideously intensified; and it came to be widely believed that one form of pressure on Roman Catholic families was the murder of Catholic children.)

***Left:** A defiant Sir Edward Carson signing the Ulster Covenant*

THE ULSTER KING-AT-ARMS
NATIONALIST
VOLUNTEERS

On 28th September 1912, at another mass meeting in Ulster, a Solemn League and Covenant was presented to the people of the north-east. In the following weeks some 220,000 men and 230,000 women are said to have signed this pledge to 'defeat the present conspiracy to set up a Home Rule Parliament in Ireland'. This, be it noted, was less than 50 per cent of the Protestant population, and less than 20 per cent of the Ulster population as a whole, even if the figures are correct, and many believe them to be greatly inflated, as such figures usually are, by persons who will vote or sign in the heat of the day but will prefer law and order to violence in the cool of the evening. However, there was certainly a great deal of very strong feeling among the Ulster Protestants. In December every signatory was asked to enrol for political, or more usually for military, service. Thus was the Ulster Volunteer Force created. They trained, at first, in civilian clothes and with dummy rifles, though by late 1913 it was estimated that there were between 50,000 and 80,000 revolvers and rifles in their hands.

1913 did nothing to improve the situation. On the first day of that year Carson, supported by Bonar Law and the Conservative Party, moved in the House of Commons that the Province of Ulster be excluded from Home Rule. Redmond would not accept this and no more would Asquith, but Asquith soon began to temporise: Home Rule would not now become effective until after the next United Kingdom general election. Redmond accepted this slippery compromise in 1914, regardless of the fact that were the Conservative Unionists to win the next general election, the Home Rule bill might never become law, while if the Liberals were to be returned they might well continue this cat-and-mouse game indefinitely. In Ireland Redmond's stock dropped several points, and *Sinn Fein* gained many new members.

In Ulster the Volunteers set about obtaining arms from abroad – Carson lunched with the Kaiser in August – and many prominent Britons, both soldiers and civilians, came out in their favour. A British general was appointed commandant of this large body of men. It became a truly military force, organised along British army lines. Finally in April 1914, 25,000 German rifles and 2,500,000 rounds of ammunition, purchased by Carson from the German government, were landed at Larne, County Antrim, and distributed rapidly to the Ulster Volunteers. The men who paraded all over Ulster and manoeuvred in the glens and mountains during the

Left: *Carson speaking. A Dubliner and Unionist, he hoped to use Ulster's unrest to prevent Home Rule anywhere in Ireland.* ***Far left:*** *Cartoons satirising Redmond* ***(top)*** *and Carson* ***(bottom)***

summer of 1914 constituted a new comparatively well-armed force in uniform, with the basic ancillary units. Although the British government at last took alarm, and by naval patrols prevented the importation of yet more weapons into Ulster, no serious attempt was made to seize those already there.

It must be noted that not all Ulster Protestants approved of Carson's and Craig's policies. A Protestant Nationalist meeting of protest had been held in County Antrim in October 1913. Among those who then spoke was Sir Roger Casement, a former British civil servant knighted for his outstanding services to humanity in the Belgian Congo and Putumayo.

In this same month of October 1913, the council of the IRB decided at a secret meeting that a counterforce to the Ulster Volunteers must be created. Furthermore Irish republicans were growing increasingly disillusioned as to the value, or even the possibility, of Home Rule. Redmond's tactics and the shilly-shallying of the British government he supported were forcing the heirs of the Fenians to look once again towards a revolutionary, as opposed to a constitutional, solution. However the men of the IRB realised that it would not be possible to set up a revolutionary armed force, and the one that they now designed was camouflaged. Eoin MacNeill, a professor of history and a political moderate, was therefore appointed chairman of a committee to raise such a force. This committee contained, deliberately, only three members of *Sinn Fein,* but a number of clandestine members of the IRB who intended effectively to control the new force. Among them was Padraic Pearse.

At the inaugural meeting in the following month MacNeill told an audience of several thousand that the Irish Volunteers were essentially a defensive force 'open to all able-bodied Irishmen without distinction of creed, politics, or social grade'. Their task would simply be to counter any attempt by the Ulster Volunteers forcibly to prevent Home Rule. At that first meeting 4,000 men enrolled, including a young teacher of mathematics and keen Gaelic linguist named Eamonn de Valera. By the end of the year the Irish Volunteers were 10,000 strong, most of them followers of John Redmond and almost all of them unarmed. They were organised on a strictly regional and local basis, company commanders, and later battalion and brigade commandants, being appointed through election.

For a short time it seemed that all Ireland save the Unionists was united behind the Irish Volunteers. **42** ▷

Right: *Ulster Volunteers around a campfire in 1914. Possibly taken on 12th July, the anniversary of the Battle of the Boyne*

The armed enemies of Home Rule

The photographs and poster on this and the next page show the preparations for resistance to Home Rule. **Below:** Carson inspecting troops of the Ulster Volunteers. This large body of men was rapidly armed and equipped with the necessary ancillary units such as signallers, a medical corps, and female auxiliaries. Far more than any branch of the Irish Volunteers, it was by August 1914 an amateur army in being. Indeed it contributed many men, often in complete units, to the Ulster Division of the British army. Characteristic of the superiority of the Ulstermen's weapons, even in the early stages of improvisation, is the machine-gun mounted on a private car **(right).** Machine-guns were rare and expensive weapons at this time. The Ulster Volunteers were armed with the almost open connivance of many British officers in defiance of their government. **Next page:** Ulster Volunteers parading with their new rifles **(left).** A pugnacious Unionist poster **(right)**

IA·435

WHO SAID WE'RE TO HAVE HOME RULE?
COME TO BELFAST AND WE'LL SHEW 'EM.

The heady prospect that Irishmen might, after all, have to fight for freedom rather than merely accept political charity from Westminster was a gust of fresh, patriotic air in the somewhat stuffy atmosphere of post-Parnell nationalism. The IRB quickly sensed this and foresaw a rebirth of Fenianism when England, as they expected she would, defaulted on Home Rule. Redmond, too, became rapidly aware of the drift and realised that the force he nominally led was in fact being manipulated by the IRB. He attempted, and theoretically succeeded, in regaining control of the Irish Volunteers in the summer of 1914 by insisting that various nominees of his own be appointed to its council. But though it did not immediately fall apart, the Volunteers were henceforth split into two unequal parts. The majority followed Redmond, the minority Padraic Pearse. In July of 1914 a small consignment of German arms was smuggled into Dublin on board Erskine Childers' yacht. These went to Pearse's men. A steady trickle of weapons was coming to them from America and other sources, but the Irish Volunteers were never as well armed as the Ulster Volunteer Force.

Thus, in 1914, there was a most anomalous situation in Ireland where no less than four private, and therefore strictly illegal, armies were marching about quite openly sometimes in uniform and often with rifles on their shoulders. There were the two wings of the Irish Volunteers (those who followed Redmond became known as the National Volunteers), there was the Ulster Volunteer Force, and there was the workers' Citizen Army.

The 'Curragh mutiny'

The overwhelming majority of British officers at this time were Conservative Unionists. Ireland has always provided a very high proportion of Britain's senior officers, many of them from Ulster. One of these was General Sir Henry Wilson, in 1914 Chief of Military Operations at the War Office and thus in a position to exert very great influence on military decisions. He was perhaps the most 'political' serving officer in the British army since Oliver Cromwell. A violent Unionist, he had immediately signed the Ulster Covenant, a direct gesture of defiance against the government of Great Britain. Nor was he alone. The Chief of the Imperial General Staff, General French, soon to become the first commander of the British Expeditionary Force in France and the Low Countries, shared his Unionist views. So too did Brigadier General Gough, a third Irishman, who in 1914 commanded the 3rd Cavalry Brigade, stationed at the Curragh Camp near Dublin, the most mobile British force available in Ireland. Their views were shared by most British officers, of all ranks, in Ireland. They regarded

Home Rule with anathema and Carson and Craig as patriots. At all levels the British army was conniving with the Ulster Volunteers in 1913 and 1914, in strict disobedience to the government which was passing the Government of Ireland Act.

The crisis came in March 1914. Orders were sent to the British commander-in-chief in Ireland, General Sir Arthur Paget, to safeguard arms depots in Ulster lest they be raided by Ulster Volunteers. Even this mild gesture against the extremists in the north-east caused a furore in the army. General Gough and many other officers threatened to resign. General Paget informed London that he could not enforce such an order, that the British army would never serve against the Ulster Unionists. Even General French threatened to resign. In Germany, where the army had for a hundred years and more obeyed its political leaders implicitly, the Kaiser decided that the British army was, as he later said, 'contemptible' and need no longer be reckoned with in the great struggle that all knew lay ahead. And in London the government capitulated to the soldiers. The Secretary of State for War, Seely, gave Gough a written assurance that the forces of the Crown would never be used to crush the opponents of Home Rule. Gough was satisfied, and French did not resign his commission. Seely, it is true, was forced to leave the War Office, but the promise remained. No serving officer was punished for 'the mutiny at the Curragh'.

This confirmed the Irish republicans in their mounting belief that the whole Home Rule promise, unsatisfactory enough if honestly intended, was in fact yet another English fraud at Ireland's expense. It was now that the Irish Volunteers began, very belatedly, to buy arms on the Continent and to garner American money and support. To more and more of his compatriots Redmond now seemed a figure in a dishonest English political game rather than an Irish leader. And when, with the outbreak of the First World War, the British government announced the postponement of Home Rule until its end – that is to say for an indefinite period once again – the IRB finally decided to abandon constitutional methods, threw its very considerable weight behind *Sinn Fein,* and decided that a rising must take place while England was in trouble and before the war was over.

A dramatic illustration of how far Redmond was now removed from the thoughts of his more activist nationalist compatriots was his suggestion, in the near hysteria that prevailed when war broke out, that Britain **50** ▷

Left: *F.E.Smith, later Lord Birkenhead, prominent English Unionist deeply involved in Irish affairs from 1912 until 1921*

The Nationalists under arms

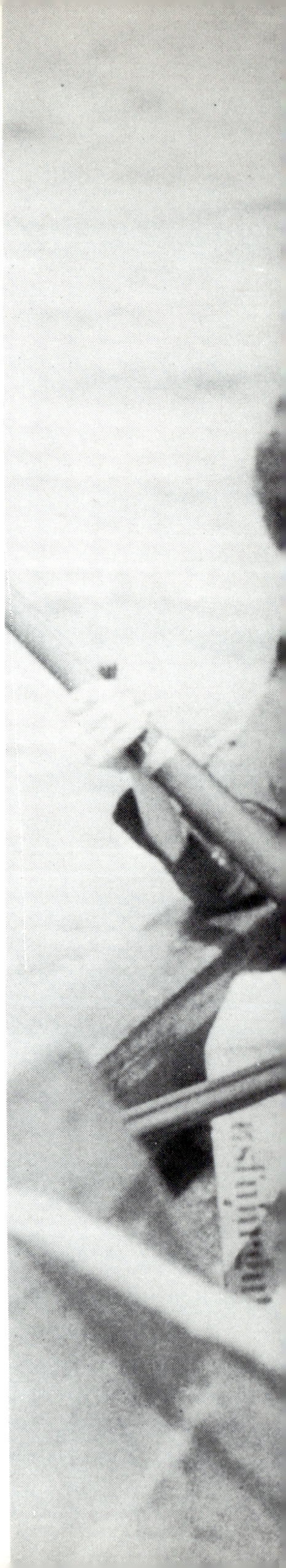

The Irish Volunteers came into existence originally as a riposte to the creation of the Ulster Volunteers. Ostensibly they were a defensive force designed to protect all Ireland, after the passage of the impending Home Rule Bill, against any attempt to overthrow Home Rule by the extremists. However, from the very beginning the IRB had envisaged the use of some Volunteers against British rule if Home Rule was not applied satisfactorily. **Below:** At first the Irish Volunteers had to train with makeshift wooden guns. **Right:** Mrs Erskine Childers and the Hon. Mary Spring Rice aboard Erskine Childers' yacht, the *Asgard,* running guns into Howth in 1914. Note ammunition boxes. **Next page:** Receiving these guns at Howth. **Following pages:** Irish Volunteers in training **(left).** A poster **(top right)** contrasting the misery of 'West Britain' with the splendours of a free 'Eire'. Sir Roger Casement with John Devoy, New York, 1914 **(centre right).** Redmond with the National Volunteers **(bottom right)**

W & M
1390
Hamburg

éIRE
WEST
BRITAIN

remove all its armed forces from Ireland and leave the policing of the country, from the military point of view, to his and the Ulster Volunteers, working in collaboration. The British government was unimpressed. It preferred to incorporate whole units of the Ulster Volunteers, as units, into the Ulster Division which fought so gallantly in France, while breaking up such units of Redmond's followers as volunteered for the Irish regiments. A great many did so, about a quarter of a million in all, including Redmond's own son who was killed in action.

This very high proportion of the young manhood of Ireland, when multiplied by their families and friends, means that the great majority of Irishmen supported Britain in the first two years of the war against Germany. British propaganda made much of the fact that Britain had gone to war in support of Belgium, a small country like Ireland. According to the English, the Irish like the Belgians must benefit from an Allied victory. The Irish were promised freedom if only they would help fight England's battles once again.

Most Irishmen accepted this argument. Though Redmond's party was moribund, the supporters of *Sinn Fein,* which became increasingly the overt political wing of the IRB, and Pearse's Irish Volunteers, who were its military wing, remained a small minority until after Easter Week 1916. Among the leaders of these Irish militants were the veteran Fenian Thomas Clarke, Sean MacDermott, and James Connolly, who was not a member of the IRB, but who, as a labour leader and head of the Citizen Army, was taken into their confidence.

During the first year and a half of the war the principal theatre in which the events to come were in preparation was outside Ireland. Casement went to America, in September 1914, to raise money, buy arms, and obtain German support for the intended rising. Many Irish-Americans were, at that time, more violently anti-British than were most of the Irish in Ireland. There were at least two reasons for this. One was that whereas the Irish in Ireland had seen thirty years of more or less benevolent British rule in their country—the Land Acts and so on—the Irish in America had either left Ireland because of the lack of opportunity there (for which they inevitably blamed the British) or were the sons or grandsons of families whose memories, handed down and losing nothing in the process, were of the really bitter years, the years of famine and of evictions. The second reason is that the Irish in Ireland were constantly rubbing shoul-

Right: *Attempting to recapture the Howth guns, the British caused many Irish casualties. The Irish Volunteers and Citizen Army attended the funeral of the 'Batchelor's Walk' victims*

ders with the English, both military and civilian, in the streets, the shops, the pubs, while a very great many Irishmen and Irishwomen had worked in England. Since the Irish, given a chance, are a tolerant, easy-going, Christian people, they could seldom regard the English they knew as the devil incarnate. The Irish-Americans could, and not infrequently did. And finally America was still neutral in a war in which ever more Irishmen were fighting alongside Englishmen. During the decade to come it was far easier to collect money for Ireland's independence in America than in Ireland itself. Apart from the reasons already given, there was more money available across the Atlantic, but furthermore a patriot who is not being asked to risk his life is more willing to open his pocket book for 'the cause'.

Casement spent a month in New York and then went on to Germany. There he attempted, with very little success, to recruit Irish prisoners-of-war for service against British rule in their own country. He refused to accept German money, a strange punctilio on the part of an active revolutionary, and seems to have attached too much importance to the Germans' promises of support and to the quasi-diplomatic treatment which he personally received as Ireland's envoy. The British in 1915 knew precisely what he was doing, since they had broken a number of German cyphers including the one which the German consul general in New York used in his communications with Berlin, the means by which Casement kept in touch with the IRB in America and, through them, with Ireland.

1915 was a comparatively quiet year, but in May a coalition government, still headed by Asquith, replaced the Liberal government. The new administration included such declared and violent Unionists as Bonar Law, F.E.Smith, Walter Long, and Edward Carson. Lord Wimborne, an old friend of Ireland's, was appointed Lord Lieutenant, and Augustine Birrell, an amiable *littérateur,* remained Chief Secretary, but this could hardly disguise the true nature of the new cabinet from the politically conscious in Ireland.

Now something close to despair descended on Redmond's followers. They knew that they had been gulled and in increasing numbers they moved across to *Sinn Fein,* but this was no longer the party that Arthur Griffith had created ten years before. It was the party of revolution, controlled by the IRB, a Fenian party, preparing for revolution at the earliest possible opportunity.

Top left: *Troops parade at the Curragh Camp near Dublin, the main British military base.* ***Bottom left:*** *British troops entrain for Belfast at the time of the so-called Curragh Mutiny.* ***Left:*** *General Sir Arthur Paget, commander-in-chief in Ireland at this time*

WE SERVE NEITHER KING NOR KAISER.
BUT IRELAND!

Chapter 4
'Keep Ireland quiet'

During 1915 casualties in the Battle of Loos, the Dardanelles, and elsewhere had depleted the strength of the British army to a level at which it could scarcely mount the offensive planned for 1916 without conscription. The great majority of potential volunteers, in England and in Ireland, had already volunteered. Therefore in January 1916 conscription became law for the whole United Kingdom, although Ireland was for the time being exempted. This caused some bitterness in Britain, particularly among left-wing pacifists many of whom went to prison rather than serve, but the vast majority accepted it as a necessary if disagreeable innovation. It seemed fair that in a great war for national survival and for democracy —for so it was presented—all Englishmen should, in theory at least, face the same risks to save their country and their chosen political system.

None of these arguments applied to Ireland. Those Irishmen who wished to help the British cause were already doing so. The rest, it may be assumed, did not, even when they were not specifically anti-British and republican. The possibility of conscription caused great unease in Ireland which the IRB believed, prematurely as it happened, could be harnessed for their purposes and should unite the people of Ireland behind *Sinn Fein*. (In fact conscription never was, and probably never could satisfactorily have been, enforced in Ireland. But it remained a threat until the end of the war. If the British government had simply excluded Ireland from the bill, this might have saved Britain many headaches to come. But the legal fiction that Ireland was an integral part of the United Kingdom prevailed over the political reality that it was a country subjected to foreign rule.)

All that spring the Volunteers marched and drilled. They even carried out a mock attack upon the General Post Office, a great fortress-like building in Sackville (now O'Connell) Street, in the heart of Dublin. On St. Patrick's Day, 17th March, reviews were held in all the principal Irish towns. The Castle, through the Special

Left: *Liberty Hall, HQ of the Irish Republican movement*

Branch and the RIC, watched these developments attentively. (At one time one Irish leader was being tagged by no less than seven detectives.) In March, Liberty Hall, the headquarters of the Irish Labour Party and of Connolly's Irish Transport and General Workers' Union, became the active headquarters of the whole Republican movement. From the end of that month it was guarded, day and night, by armed men of the Citizen Army. And on 28th March the Volunteers' executive council announced that any attempt by the government to deprive the Volunteers of their arms would be resisted by force. The Chief Commissioner of Police urged that such a step be taken nonetheless, but the Chief Secretary and the Under-Secretary were unwilling to precipitate a rising which they hoped would never come. Nor had they sufficient evidence at this time to arrest the Republican leaders and keep them in prison.

But the Rising had been decided upon. Casement was about to sail from Germany with the necessary guns, and on 3rd April Padraic Pearse, commandant of the Volunteers, issued an order that the whole force was to be prepared for three days of manoeuvres over the Easter weekend. Easter that year fell on 23rd April. Indeed the IRB leaders who were planning the Rising had decided as long ago as January that it was to take place on that date, though this information was not then passed to Eoin MacNeill, chairman of the Volunteers' executive council and also their chief-of-staff, nor to the other moderates even when, like MacNeill and Hobson, they were themselves members of the IRB. This was a conspiracy within a conspiracy.

The plan was a complex one, inevitably. It also required a precision of timing from which regular staff officers, with a full system of military communications at their disposal, might well have recoiled. And a communications network was precisely what the conspirators lacked. They could not even use the fairly efficient Volunteers' network since it was their intention not to inform MacNeill until the very latest possible moment. Even so MacNeill was suspicious and exacted a promise from Pearse, Ceannt (Kent), and MacDonagh that they would issue no orders, other than routine ones, to the Volunteers without his personal endorsement. This promise they gave, though they had no intention of keeping it. They were well aware that MacNeill and most of his executive council were opposed to a rising at this time. They knew that MacNeill had the power to countermand it, as had Hobson. They hoped that once it was launched the logic of events would

Far right: *Many Irishmen responded to British exhortations to enlist, but others joined the Irish Volunteers instead* ***(right)***

"I'll go too!"
THE
REAL IRISH SPIRIT.

FOR THE GLORY OF IRELAND
BELGIUM
'WILL YOU GO OR MUST I'?

sweep the moderates, and indeed the whole Volunteer Army, along with the insurgents.

It was planned that Casement would land the German guns and his Irish recruits from the prisoner-of-war camps in Tralee Bay on Good Friday if possible and no earlier than Thursday or later than Saturday. The guns would then be very rapidly distributed in Limerick, Cork, and throughout the west and south. The whole of the Volunteer Army there and in Dublin was to rise on Sunday evening, when an Irish Republic would be declared. Key points in the cities were to be seized, the RIC and the British military taken by surprise and whenever possible disarmed.

The capture of Casement

If communications within Ireland were difficult, those with Casement were infinitely more so. On 6th April he received a message from Joseph Plunkett, an IRB leader close to Pearse, who had managed to get to Switzerland. Plunkett now told Casement, and for the first time, the date was fixed; the German arms must be brought ashore in Tralee Bay not later than dawn on Easter Saturday; it was essential that German officers be sent to serve with the Irish Republican Army; a German submarine was required at the same time in the port of Dublin.

Casement was now close to despair. The Germans could not send officers at such short notice, nor were they prepared to risk a U-boat in Dublin Bay. Instead of two arms ships, as originally agreed with Casement, they decided to send only one, the *Aud*. Casement did not believe it would penetrate the British naval blockade. He therefore decided he could not risk the lives of his Irish prisoners-of-war, who, if captured, would certainly be shot for high treason. In fact he did not believe that the Rising could succeed or should be attempted at that time.

On 9th April the *Aud*, flying Norwegian colours, sailed. There was no Irishman on board. Casement's only contact with the leaders in Ireland was by German cypher via the United States. To use this for the purpose he now desired would inform the German government that he was now urging the Irish to abandon a project in which he personally had embroiled the Germans. He felt that the Germans had let him down—he was under great strain at this time—and must have doubted if they would even let such a message through. He therefore decided that he must himself go to Ireland, and the Germans agreed to transport him by U-boat. He intended to meet the *Aud* in Tralee Bay, in the unlikely event of her ever arriving there. Whether she did or not, he could warn the IRB and persuade them to call off the Rising. Alternatively his own capture by the British should serve

as a warning to the Irish leaders that the now hopeless insurrection must be postponed. In Ireland's history there is even more paradox than in the annals of most lands. Casement, an Irish patriot, was to be hanged by the British later in the year because he had attempted, single-handed, to stop an insurrection by other Irish patriots against British rule.

In Ireland the leaders of the Rising realised, belatedly, that Easter always falls on the first Sunday after a full moon. It might well be impossible to land and distribute the German weapons under cover of darkness. Therefore they must arrive at the last possible moment, so that the moon would be further on the wane, and so that the RIC would have less time to search for the weapons once they were ashore. Furthermore the date of the Rising had been postponed to Easter Monday—for the somewhat superficial reason that a race meeting at Fairyhouse on that day was likely to attract many officers of the British garrison out of Dublin. Therefore a message was sent to Berlin, via New York, that the guns must be landed on Sunday night and not as previously arranged. The *Aud* was on the high seas, circumnavigating the northern tip of Scotland, and had no wireless. Her captain, who had skilfully made his way through the British naval blockade and one of the worst gales of the century, sailed into Tralee Bay on Thursday afternoon, the earliest permitted time in the only orders he had ever received. There was no one there to meet him. That night there was no green signal light from the shore. The British knew all about the *Aud* and were waiting for it. He waited for twenty-four hours. On Friday afternoon ships of the Royal Navy arrived. He was ordered to proceed to Queenstown, now Cobh, where he blew up his ship before entering the port. So none of the guns he carried ever reached the men of Easter Week.

That same Thursday evening Casement and two companions landed from the U-boat in Tralee Bay. They had seen the *Aud* riding at anchor, but had thought it unwise to hail her. Casement, exhausted, was left in a field while his companions tried to find the Republican emissaries from Dublin of whom Austin Stack was the most important. Casement was arrested that same night.

One of Casement's companions, Robert Monteith, managed on Friday to send a messenger to Dublin with a note explaining what had happened to Casement and saying that if the Rising were dependent on German arms it should now be called off. Addressed to MacNeill, who Monteith assumed was fully informed, it was in fact delivered to Connolly at Liberty Hall, who told Pearse.

Left: *A tram covered with recruiting posters rolls through Dublin*

On that same Friday Pearse had seen MacNeill in the morning. The previous day MacNeill, quite uninformed about Casement and the *Aud,* had realised that a rising was imminent. He was angered by this breach of promise on the part of Pearse and his faction. He therefore dismissed several senior officers of the Volunteers and replaced them with men of his own views. Now Pearse told him, in all good faith, that German arms were about to come ashore, and that the Rising was to take place on Monday. Reluctantly MacNeill played the part that Pearse had assigned him, and agreed that the whole force of Volunteers support the Rising, actively when armed, passively when not. But still the insurrectionists were taking no chances. They arrested Bulmer Hobson, an IRB member of sufficient seniority in the Volunteers to have countermanded Pearse's orders. This was perhaps the first act in the civil war that then lay far ahead.

On Saturday morning the news reached Dublin of Casement's arrest and the destruction of the *Aud.* MacNeill went into reverse, immediately and violently. He cancelled all manoeuvres by the Irish Volunteers that weekend, even inserting a notice to this effect in *The Sunday Independent* and, so far as he could, informing outlying companies by runner.

Early on Sunday morning the Military Council, that is to say Pearse's principal lieutenants and allies, met at Liberty Hall. Thomas Clarke presided. Despite the disasters in Kerry, despite MacNeill's order, despite the now hopeless nature of the whole undertaking, they decided that the Rising would take place on the following day and, so far as possible, as planned. Thomas MacDonagh, commandant of the Dublin brigade, issued an order, countersigned by Padraic Pearse, that his four battalions would parade at 10 am on Monday morning. It was also decided that since Liberty Hall must be the prime target for any British counterattack, it should be evacuated. Connolly agreed. He and his Citizen Army fully supported Pearse and the Military Council.

The reactions of the British authorities, in London and even more so in Dublin, were strange in so far as they were almost nonexistent. When the Rising took place many British officers were, as anticipated, at the Fairyhouse race meeting: the Secretary, Augustine Birrell, was in London and the General Officer Commanding the British army in Ireland was also away from his command post: only the Lord Lieutenant, Lord Wimborne, who had known Ireland well for many years, seems to have been sufficiently worried by possible, immediate developments to have cancelled a trip to Belfast arranged for Easter

Right: *The Citizen Army parades openly in full uniform, 1915*

Sunday. Indeed on that evening he was telling the Under-Secretary, Sir Matthew Nathan – in Birrell's absence the actual head of the administration, as Wimborne was the titular – that he wanted 'between sixty and a hundred of the ringleaders arrested tonight'. Nathan disagreed. Nobody was arrested. To do so would have meant an armed attack on the Citizen Army. Yet at first glance it seems to be the political equivalent of Conan Doyle's Sherlock Holmes mystery: the dog that did not bark in the night. Why did it not bark?

The answer is complex and tentative. Certain facts are established, certain theories untenable.

One fact is that the British government in London did not inform Dublin Castle about the German arms ship, nor about the U-boat carrying Casement to Ireland (if this was known in London) until the ship had been blown up and Casement captured. This is explicable. Cypher-breaking in the First and Second World Wars was an extremely secret business. The dissemination of intelligence from this source was limited to the minimum of recipients, and then the source was usually disguised. To have informed Dublin that the *Aud* had sailed would have given away the source of this intelligence, were the Germans aware that British Naval Intelligence knew of the sailing: it was improbable that any spy could have got the intelligence across in the time: security at Dublin Castle was notoriously lax: on the other hand for the *Aud* to be intercepted by a British warship was a normal hazard of war. Therefore had London informed Dublin about the *Aud,* and perhaps about Casement too, and had this information got back to Germany, it was probable that the German security services would have immediately changed their cyphers, in particular their diplomatic cypher to America and their naval cypher, both of which were being read by British Naval Intelligence to very, very great advantage. This was a period when it was of the utmost value to the British that they should be 'listening in' to German-American relations from the German point of view. The Battles of Jutland and of the Somme also were only a few weeks ahead, and each of these might have been decisive to the outcome of the war one way or the other. Compared to this major struggle Ireland appeared a side-show, though an important one, to the British and the Germans alike. That was why the German admiralty had not given Casement all the support he desired. And that was also why the British admiralty merely informed the appropriate naval commander who arranged the interception of the *Aud.*

The failure to inform Dublin Castle was not, as has been suggested, an example of inefficiency on the part of British intelligence, but rather the contrary. The intelli-

gence officers concerned could hardly be expected to foresee the huge and lasting political implications in the rise of a few hundred desperate Irish republicans; they could and did see the huge battles looming in the main theatre of war both on sea and on land: far better to risk a few deaths in Ireland than the loss of these; and for these, the ability to read German cyphers might well prove of vital importance. Thus, immediately before the Rising, Dublin Castle lacked the key piece to the jigsaw, even though this was now known in London. The Castle had to rely on its own intelligence.

Too much and too little intelligence

The theory has been advanced that the British wished the Rising to take place, in order to crush it with the utmost brutality, cow the Irish into total submission, and destroy the possibility of Home Rule forever. This may well have been true of certain extreme Unionists in London, Belfast, and elsewhere. It was certainly not true so far as the most responsible members of the British cabinet were concerned. Their eyes, like those of their intelligence officers, were on the main struggle with Germany, and they wished for no disturbance in the rear. No more was this true of Dublin Castle, where the administration had explicit and implicit orders to 'keep Ireland quiet', orders which they were obviously, if inexpertly, attempting to carry out. This counter-conspiratorial myth was, in fact, no more than a traumatic echo of the identical, and equally unfounded, myth that the British had somehow manipulated the Irish into the rising of 1798 in order to destroy Irish nationalism and enforce an Act of Union.

Still, why did the Castle do nothing in the weeks and days before the Easter Rising? There is no complete answer, but only a number of partial ones:

Various illegal and semi-armed private Irish armies had been marching about the country and parading in the cities for several years. By the spring of 1916 they had become part of the normal Irish scene. Since the Irish like to mock, 'Slatter's Mounted Foot' was a good joke, and all this military activity not to be taken too seriously.

The intelligence network was too big and too indiscriminate. The number of reports reaching Dublin Castle each day must have been enormous, both from the Special Branch and from the RIC. The evaluation of such reports is of considerably greater importance than their collection. The evaluation section in the Castle was understaffed, and it is fair to assume that the best British intelligence officers were engaged, in 1916, on more im-

Left: *Casement, centre, aboard U-19 on the way to Ireland* portant tasks—from the British point of view—than evaluating the views of the police chief in Skibbereen or the political situation in West Mayo. Furthermore the garrulousness and love of gossip of the Irish must have made the sifting of such intelligence extremely difficult: warnings that there were 'thousands of armed men in the hills' and that 'a rebellion is on us to-morrow' must have been pouring into the Castle from all corners of the country for years now. Too much intelligence produces a cloud of ink.

At a more important level there was too little intelligence. The Specials seem to have had small success in infiltrating the real and fighting leadership of the IRB, of the Citizen Army, or of *Sinn Fein*. Where truly serious matters are concerned the Irish can be remarkably reticent. As with the Jews, centuries of persecution had handed on, from generation to generation, the knowledge of when and how silence is vital. Persecuted people breed superb conspirators: in 1916 the British had not been so persecuted for some eight centuries, and did not understand the technique.

The Special Branch must have had some success, however, to provide Lord Wimborne's outburst to Sir Matthew Nathan. Sir Matthew's bland disagreement with his 'constitutional monarch's' diagnosis and proposed course of action is explicable in three ways.

In the first place he knew that Liberty Hall had been, for some time now, a building guarded by armed men. To seize this large number of Irish leaders would have certainly entailed a military assault upon it supported by artillery. This would almost surely have precipitated the rising which it was his duty to prevent.

Secondly, he was an experienced soldier, colonial administrator, and Whitehall civil servant. A lieutenant-colonel in the Royal Engineers, he had subsequently governed Sierra Leone, the Gold Coast, and Hong Kong, before becoming Chairman of the Board of Inland Revenue. He was sent to his present job in Ireland in 1914. Thus his was not a background likely to impart intuitive understanding of revolutionary fervours and lost causes. He worked at his desk. He handled facts. From these facts he drew the logical deductions. He must, being a clever man, have assumed that his Irish opponents were as clever and as logical as was he, not at all like the near savages of the Gold Coast. He did not know Ireland or the Irish—apart from Dublin Castle society—at all well. For many years now he had been dealing with pieces of paper rather than with men. To a clever, conscientious, upright, and highly efficient British civil servant of that age, and perhaps of this, emotional entanglement was the direct opposite of clear thought. Cer-

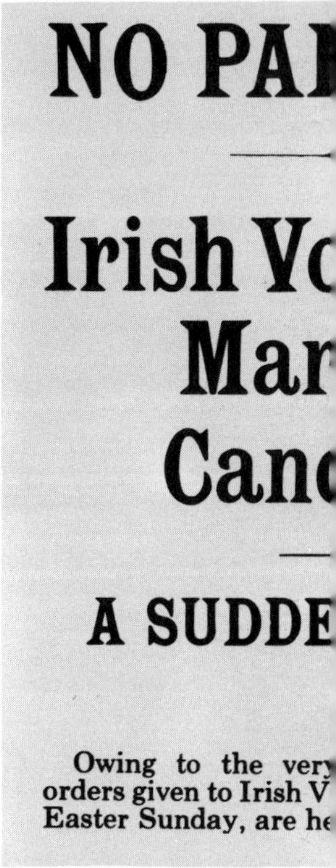

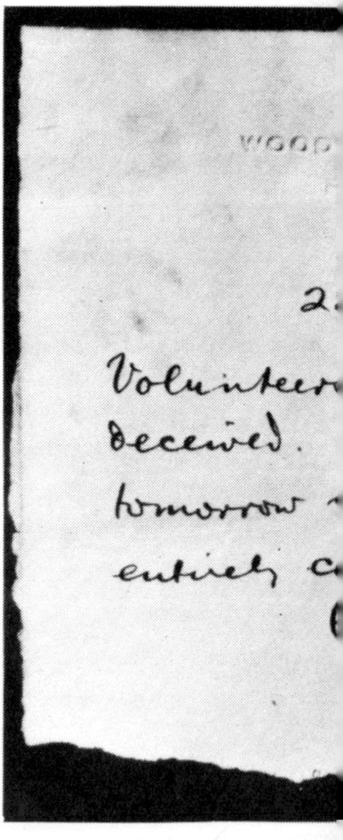

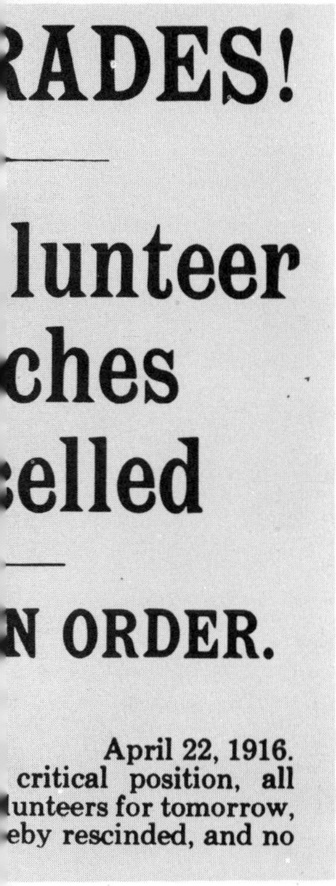

RADES!

lunteer
ches
elled

N ORDER.

April 22, 1916.
critical position, all
lunteers for tomorrow,
eby rescinded, and no

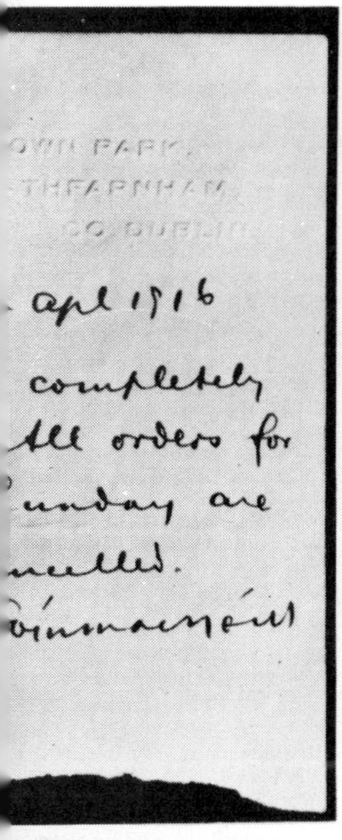

apl 1916
completely
All orders for
unday are
ncelled.

tain actions can be expected to produce certain results. Without the German guns, probably even with them, an Irish insurrection could lead only to direct and immediate disaster for the rebels. Therefore, according to a highly intelligent man such as Nathan, highly intelligent men such as MacNeill, Pearse, Hobson, and Connolly would not commit personal and national suicide. As was to be shown, he was half right.

Thirdly, he knew about the split within the leadership of the Volunteers. MacNeill's cancellation of the so-called manoeuvres made the prospect of a successful rising nil. The extremists could only rely on a few hundred men, scantily armed. Even if from Sir Matthew Nathan's point of view Clarke, Pearse, Connolly, and their supporters were fanatics, he would certainly not have regarded them as madmen. Yet from his, and not only from his, viewpoint, a rising on Easter Monday must be an act of madness. Therefore he assumed that it would not take place.

And so no special precautions were taken by the British: nobody was recalled from leave: and on Easter Monday a large number of British officers left Dublin to go to the races at Fairyhouse.

Padraic Pearse was well aware that the Easter Rising was suicidal, personally, but he hoped and believed that nationally it would have an exactly opposite effect. Before ever it happened he said to his mother: 'The day is coming when I shall be shot, swept away, and my colleagues like me.' When his mother enquired about her other son, William, who served in the Volunteers under Padraic, he is said to have replied: 'William? Shot like the others. We'll all be shot.' And James Connolly is reported to have remarked: 'The chances against us are a thousand to one.' On the morning of the Rising, when asked by one of his men if there was no hope, he replied cheerfully: 'None whatever!'

It was hard for the staff officers and the civil servants of Dublin Castle, accustomed to weighing possibilities so far as their own actions were concerned, to realise that a group of men, perhaps some 1,250 strong (including some 250 men of the Citizen Army who took no notice of MacNeill), was prepared to fight and die in such circumstances. They should have been wiser in their age: the slaughter at Ypres was recent, Verdun was going on, the Somme about to happen. Seldom in history have men been so willing, indeed so eager, to throw away their lives for an ideal, almost any ideal, and the Irish ideal had deep, long roots. The men went out, and fought, and died.

Left:** MacNeill's attempts to call off the Rising: the notice in* The Sunday Independent ***(top)** and a scribbled note **(bottom)

Chapter 5

The Easter Rising

There was not time to change the proposed military operation between Friday and Monday, though its scope was now so reduced that its nature was basically altered. Instead of seizing key points in the cities, controlling road and rail communications, and fighting the main battles in the mountains, it now became apparent that the battle must be fought, immediately, in Dublin itself where MacDonagh's brigade and the Citizen Army were the principal forces on which Pearse could rely, about 1,000 of the former and some 250 of the latter. The hastily modified plan was to hold the seized buildings for as long as possible and thus to disrupt British control of the capital. It was then hoped that one of three things might happen: the rest of the Volunteers, and indeed the country in general, might rise in sympathy despite MacNeill; the British might realise the danger of alienating the United States at this critical moment of the war, and being also made aware of the ultimate impossibility of holding Ireland down by force, would pull out voluntarily; and last and faintest of hopes, the Germans might still somehow come to the rescue of the rebels. Since the rebels had no artillery of any sort, their strongpoints could only hold out provided that the British did not use theirs. Connolly hoped that the British, for capitalist reasons, would not bombard Dublin and thus destroy their own – or largely their own – property. This, too, was an illusion.

H-hour was 12 noon and since this was a Bank Holiday there were crowds in the streets who witnessed the small bodies of Volunteers and of the Citizen Army marching, armed, through the city to seize their various strongpoints. It went, on the whole, remarkably smoothly. Five major buildings or groups of buildings were seized north of the River Liffey, nine south of it, and some of the railway stations were occupied. Headquarters were established as planned in the massive General Post Office, from which Irish flags were flown and where Padraic Pearse announced the creation of a provisional government for the new Irish Republic and nailed up a proclamation to this

Left: *British troops fire behind a barricade, Easter Week 1916*

effect. With him in the Post Office were Connolly as military commander, Tom Clarke, Joseph Plunkett (a very sick man who had come straight from a nursing home), the O'Rahilly, Sean MacDermott, and other leaders. There, too, was a young soldier by the name of Michael Collins. The rebels immediately set about preparing the Post Office against the attack which they expected to be launched almost at once.

The four other principal strongpoints seized were the South Dublin Union, a collection of poorhouses and the like (Eamonn Ceannt); the Four Courts, normally the centre of the legal profession, where heavy law books were used as sandbags (Eamonn Daly); St Stephen's Green, where trenches were dug and barricades of motorcars erected (Michael Mallin and the Countess Markievicz, herself in officer's uniform); and Boland's Flour Mill, which covered the approach roads from Dun Laoghaire, then called Kingstown, where any reinforcements sent from England would almost certainly disembark (Eamonn de Valera). An attempt was made to seize Dublin Castle. The leader of the Irish force sent to capture it had overestimated the size of the British detachment there, which was in fact negligible. Since his own force was far below the strength he had anticipated, he did not rush the defenders. When fired upon, his men withdrew to nearby buildings and sniped. An ingenious plan to capture a large quantity of arms and ammunition from the arsenal in Phoenix Park known as the Magazine Fort was also only partly successful—the British officer in command had gone off to the races, with the key in his pocket, instead of hanging it up in its usual place: only a small number of rifles were seized, and a boy was killed lest he give the alarm. On the other hand telephone lines were successfully cut, though again owing to the shortage of men not to the extent planned. Still, Dublin Castle was for a time almost isolated. A further success was that a troop of Lancers which attempted to charge down Sackville Street was repulsed with casualties from the Post Office, and withdrew.

The British had been taken by surprise and were almost completely in the dark as to the scale and the scope of the Rising. The Castle immediately ordered up troops from the Curragh and the other camps outside Dublin, and also appealed to London for reinforcements. There Lord French, that violent Irish Unionist and a man of unstable temperament, was Commander-in-Chief, British Forces in the United Kingdom, having been relieved of his appointment as Commander-in-Chief, British Expeditionary Force. His reaction was immediate and exaggerated. He ordered that no less than four divisions—when at full strength and with ancillary troops some 100,000 men, sorely needed on the Western Front—be alerted for transfer to Ireland. Just as Irish policy alternated between constitutional and revolutionary methods, so English policy changed, and was to change again more than once, between appeasement and suppression. Though the mass of the Irish people, as of the English, did not then know it, Home Rule, real or sham, died on Easter Monday 1916, and with it died Redmond's Irish Nationalist Party. A very small minority of Irishmen had chosen violence. The British government knew the steps in this *danse macabre*. The Irish rebels were to be crushed, rapidly and massively. But those Irish rebels also knew that the dance would go on after their death. That was why they had risen against such odds.

The atrocities begin

From a military point of view Tuesday was comparatively calm. But if the English in Dublin were in the dark, so too were the rebels. They had no wireless links between the strongpoints they had seized, nor with the outside world. Communication was by runner, usually the boys of *Fianna na hEireann,* and this became increasingly difficult and eventually impossible as fighting reached its peak.

British strategy, hastily improvised, was to throw a cordon around that area of Dublin where the rebels held their strongpoints, then cut that area in two, and finally mop up. For this purpose Trinity College, with its strong buildings and extensive walled grounds, was tactically of great value, being in the very centre of the city and with a command of the principal bridge over the Liffey. The original plan of the Irish Republicans had included Trinity among points to be seized, but a shortage of manpower had made this impossible. Trinity was academically the centre of Unionist thought. Officer cadets were in training there for service with the British army. It would not have surrendered as did the Post Office and the other occupied buildings, and Pearse did not have enough men to attack its complex of buildings behind their long, high walls. Its great gate was closed against the rebels, and only opened when the British guns and British soldiers arrived.

On Tuesday, too, looting increased and martial law was declared. British reinforcements were arriving at Kingstown. A mad British officer, a certain Captain Bowen-Colthurst, had three harmless Irish journalists shot 'while trying to escape'—a euphemism to become hide-

Left: *Some of the leaders of the Easter Rising: Padraic Pearse* ***(top left),*** *Thomas Clarke* ***(top right),*** *Joseph Plunkett* ***(upper centre left),*** *Eamonn Daly* ***(upper centre right),*** *Sean MacDermott* ***(lower centre left),*** *Eamonn Ceannt* ***(lower centre right),*** *James Connolly* ***(bottom left),*** *Thomas MacDonagh* ***(bottom right)***

ously familiar, and not only in Ireland. One of these was a well-known Dublin figure named Sheehy-Skeffington, a feminist and pacifist. The atrocities had begun. Some 18-pounder guns had now reached the British army from Athlone and with these they began to shell Liberty Hall, inhabited only by its caretaker.

By Wednesday morning the rebels were already outnumbered twenty to one. The British now began to attack in earnest. The gunboat HMS *Helga* sailed up the Liffey and set about the destruction of Liberty Hall by shellfire. The naval gunfire was inaccurate, as was that of the army's artillery, many other buildings were hit and set on fire, and many civilians killed. Connolly had been wrong: a shell from a 9-pounder gun was used to kill a single sniper near Dublin Castle. Dublin began to burn, and Dubliners to starve, for there was no food coming into the city. This was no longer a police action but full-scale war, in which no attempt was made to spare the civilians. Meanwhile British reinforcements marching in from Kingstown were ambushed by de Valera's men and suffered heavy casualties, but at last by dint of numbers forced their way through. St Stephen's Green had been cleared of rebels, who retreated into the Royal College of Surgeons where they established a strongpoint.

On Thursday the new British commander-in-chief arrived. Since all Ireland was now under martial law, he held full powers there. General Sir John Maxwell was a soldier of some distinction who had returned the month before from Egypt, where he had been commander-in-chief of the Anglo-Egyptian armies for some years. Although he numbered the Countess Markievicz among his cousins he had no knowledge or understanding of the political mood in Ireland. Indeed in the months to come he was to do more to undermine British rule in Ireland than all the rebels put together. He had been ordered by Asquith to put down the rebellion with all possible speed and by all the means at his disposal. This he proceeded to do, regardless of political consequences.

The reinforcements from England were now in action. These were in large measure untrained and inexperienced soldiers, being asked to engage in the sort of fighting that all soldiers find loathsome. They soon discovered that many of the men in the Irish Republican Army, as the rebel forces now called themselves, lacked uniforms and fought in civilian clothes. The British soldiers did not therefore always wait to see if a man running 75 ▷

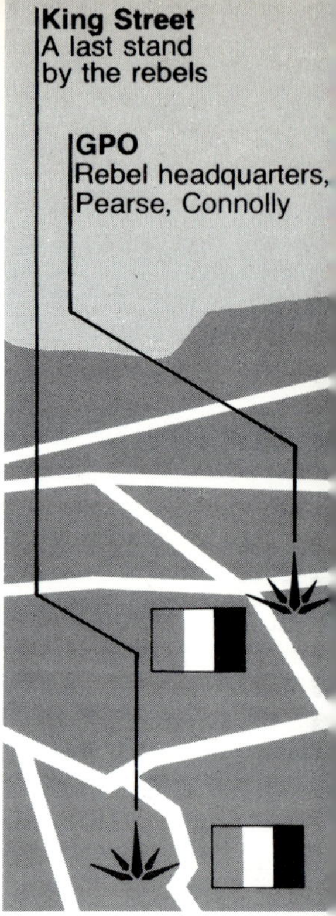

***Top right:** Dublin in 1916 showing the main strongholds held by the Irish, both Pearse's Volunteers and Connolly's Citizen Army. **Bottom:** British troops in action against a rebel strongpoint. **Next page:** Joseph McGill's painting of the Easter Rising*

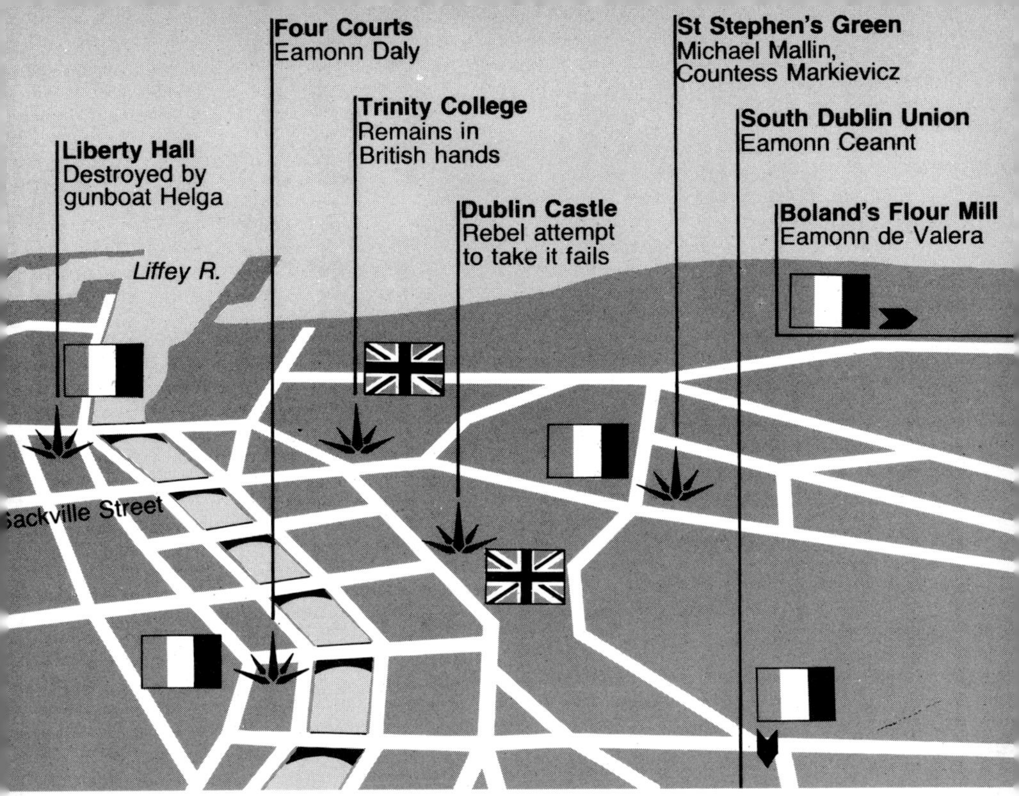
Four Courts
Eamonn Daly
St Stephen's Green
Michael Mallin,
Countess Markievicz
Trinity College
Remains in
British hands
South Dublin Union
Eamonn Ceannt
Liberty Hall
Destroyed by
gunboat Helga
Dublin Castle
Rebel attempt
to take it fails
Boland's Flour Mill
Eamonn de Valera
Liffey R.
Sackville Street

BROOKS

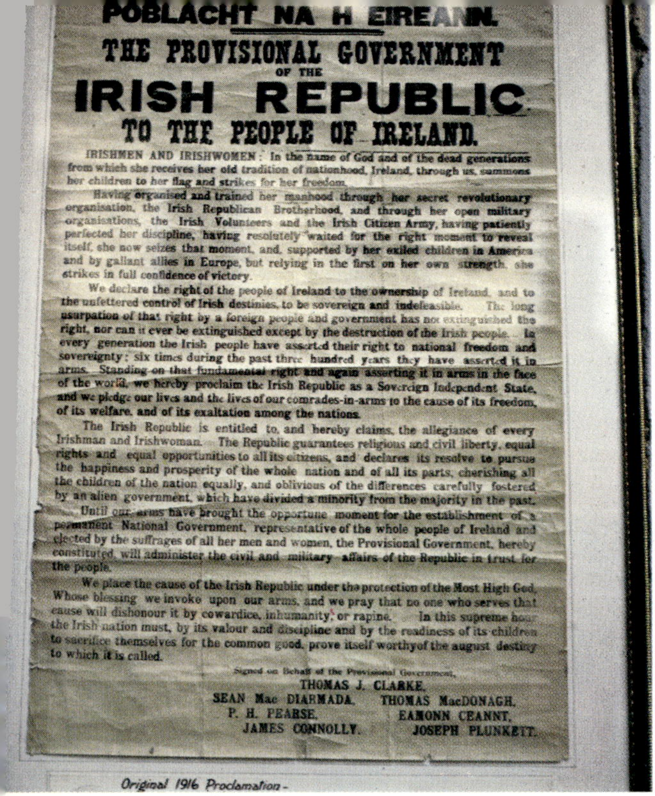

POBLACHT NA H EIREANN.

THE PROVISIONAL GOVERNMENT
OF THE
IRISH REPUBLIC
TO THE PEOPLE OF IRELAND.

IRISHMEN AND IRISHWOMEN: In the name of God and of the dead generations from which she receives her old tradition of nationhood, Ireland, through us, summons her children to her flag and strikes for her freedom.

Having organised and trained her manhood through her secret revolutionary organisation, the Irish Republican Brotherhood, and through her open military organisations, the Irish Volunteers and the Irish Citizen Army, having patiently perfected her discipline, having resolutely waited for the right moment to reveal itself, she now seizes that moment, and, supported by her exiled children in America and by gallant allies in Europe, but relying in the first on her own strength, she strikes in full confidence of victory.

We declare the right of the people of Ireland to the ownership of Ireland, and to the unfettered control of Irish destinies, to be sovereign and indefeasible. The long usurpation of that right by a foreign people and government has not extinguished the right, nor can it ever be extinguished except by the destruction of the Irish people. In every generation the Irish people have asserted their right to national freedom and sovereignty; six times during the past three hundred years they have asserted it in arms. Standing on that fundamental right and again asserting it in arms in the face of the world, we hereby proclaim the Irish Republic as a Sovereign Independent State, and we pledge our lives and the lives of our comrades-in-arms to the cause of its freedom, of its welfare, and of its exaltation among the nations.

The Irish Republic is entitled to, and hereby claims, the allegiance of every Irishman and Irishwoman. The Republic guarantees religious and civil liberty, equal rights and equal opportunities to all its citizens, and declares its resolve to pursue the happiness and prosperity of the whole nation and of all its parts, cherishing all the children of the nation equally, and oblivious of the differences carefully fostered by an alien government, which have divided a minority from the majority in the past.

Until our arms have brought the opportune moment for the establishment of a permanent National Government, representative of the whole people of Ireland and elected by the suffrages of all her men and women, the Provisional Government, hereby constituted, will administer the civil and military affairs of the Republic in trust for the people.

We place the cause of the Irish Republic under the protection of the Most High God, Whose blessing we invoke upon our arms, and we pray that no one who serves that cause will dishonour it by cowardice, inhumanity, or rapine. In this supreme hour the Irish nation must, by its valour and discipline and by the readiness of its children to sacrifice themselves for the common good, prove itself worthy of the august destiny to which it is called.

Signed on Behalf of the Provisional Government,
THOMAS J. CLARKE.
SEAN Mac DIARMADA. THOMAS MacDONAGH.
P. H. PEARSE. EAMONN CEANNT.
JAMES CONNOLLY. JOSEPH PLUNKETT.

Original 1916 Proclamation -

across a street was armed before firing at him. Furthermore the rifles that had been run into Howth by Erskine Childers in 1914 were of German make purchased originally by the Russians and firing the soft-nosed or 'dum dum' bullet which had been condemned by the Hague Convention. The Russians had disposed of these 'illegal' weapons to a German arms merchant, who had sold them to the Irish. A soft-nosed bullet makes a very hideous wound; the Boers had been accused of atrocity for using them sixteen years before; now, as it seemed to the soldiers, these armed civilians were murdering their comrades in a particularly foul way. And they began shooting civilians at sight. The worst offenders were the men of the South Staffordshire Regiment.

On that day attacks were made on Boland's Mill, the men in the South Dublin Union were forced to give ground, and there was fairly intensive shelling of the General Post Office, which began to burn from the top down. Connolly was wounded twice. The first wound he hid from his men: the second was more serious, one foot was shattered, and he was in great pain. With the aid of morphia he carried on, directing the battle as best he could. The Dublin fires were now great conflagrations, comparable to those that raged in London at the height of the Blitz of 1940-1941. With the streets crosscut by small-arms fire and the water supply a mere trickle, these could not be dealt with. The British now encircled central Dublin tightly and, using Trinity College as a base, split the strongpoints north of the river from those on the south side. Still no major rebel strongpoint surrendered.

On Friday Connolly ordered the women who had fought so bravely to leave the General Post Office, which was now cut off and burning. Later that day he and Pearse and the other survivors who had marched there on Monday escaped from a building that was almost red-hot and about to collapse. They found temporary refuge nearby, while the British continued to shell the empty, burning building. A last battle was fought for King's Street, near the Four Courts. It took some 5,000 British soldiers, equipped with armoured cars and artillery, twenty-eight hours to advance about 150 yards against some 200 rebels almost all of whom had been fighting, without sleep, for five days. It was then that the South Staffs bayonetted and shot civilians hiding in cellars.

All was over. On Saturday morning Pearse and Connolly surrendered unconditionally. By their orders, **83** ▷

Top left: *After the Rising was crushed, all the signatories to the Proclamation of the Irish Republic were executed.* ***Bottom left:*** *British troops.* ***Left:*** *Outside the Four Courts.* ***Next page:*** *British troops search a car during the bitter fighting*

MERCHANT

'A Terrible Beauty is Born'

It had been hoped by Connolly, operational commander of the Irish forces, that the British would refrain from using artillery. As a Marxist he believed somewhat naively that British capitalists would not permit British guns to destroy what was largely British property. He was wrong. The British employed all the weapons at their immediate disposal, including a gunboat and armoured cars, to crush the Rising. Little if any attempt was made to spare the civilian population, the majority of whom were at this time opposed to Pearse, Connolly, and their followers. Dublin was treated like a battlefield, like any battlefield of the First World War on which an artillery barrage preceded an infantry attack **(right** and **below)**. One result of these tactics was that some 2,000 Irishmen were able to resist a force eventually some thirty times as large, for almost a week. Another was that large areas of Dublin were reduced to rubble as is vividly shown in this painting by Joseph McGill **(next page)**

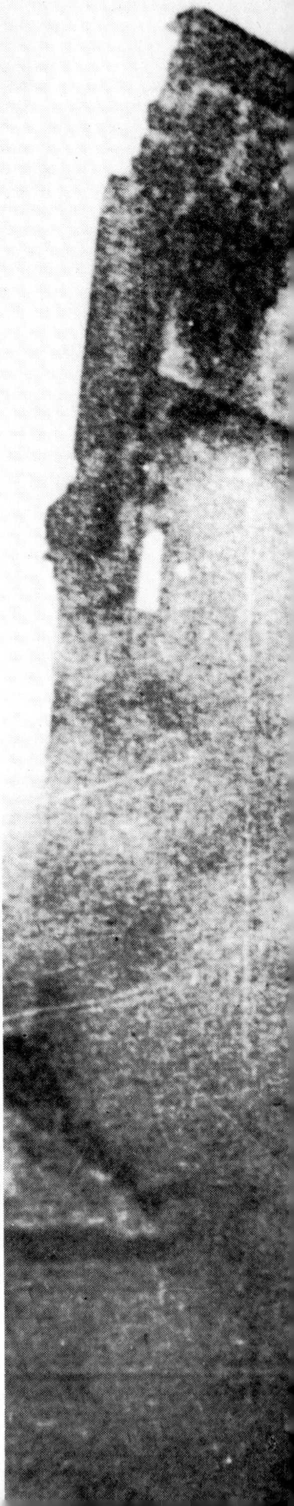

conveyed through the British military, the other strongpoints followed suit.

Like so much else about the Easter Rising, casualties are hard to estimate. It would seem that those of the British were about 500, those of the Irish, including civilians, about twice that figure. Material damage has been estimated at about £2,500,000 ($12,000,000) in the currency of the time. Large parts of Dublin lay in ruins. (These blunt statistics, though, must be seen in the proportions of the time. A few weeks later the Battle of the Somme was launched, where it has been estimated that British casualties amounted to 20,000 dead on the first day, and 419,654 dead before it finally failed to break the German front, while most of the cities of northern France and southern Belgium were already partly or entirely in ruins.)

When, on Sunday, the Irishmen who had surrendered were marched across Dublin from one prison compound to another, they were at times jeered at and booed by the crowds, particularly in the slum areas. In the countryside the Rising had received only minimal support. Public opinion had been against the Rising before it began, throughout Easter Week, and remained so after its defeat, until the reprisals began.

On the direct orders of the Cabinet in London these were swift, secret, and brutal. The leaders were tried by court martial and shot: only when they were dead were their condemnations to death announced and their families informed. Among those thus killed were Willie Pearse, who was no leader and who, it was generally believed in Ireland, was killed because he was Padraic's brother; the old Fenian, Thomas Clarke; the invalid Plunkett; and, most disgusting to all Irish minds, Connolly, who was in any case dying, and had to be propped up in bed for the court martial in his hospital room. He was shot in a chair since he could no longer stand. A wave of disgust swept across Ireland: nor was it diminished by Asquith's acceptance of responsibility for these measures in the House of Commons.

It was increased by the state trial of Sir Roger Casement, held in London only a few weeks later, under the Treason Act of 1351. That act, written in Norman French and lacking commas, is subject to two legal interpretations. The principal prosecuting counsel for the Crown was F. E. Smith, who had been a close colleague of Carson and remained a highly important Unionist politician. The whole trial thus developed an intensely political

Left: *Destruction in Dublin after the Rising. At first, the men who had fought were booed in the streets, and it was not until the executions began that public opinion began to turn*

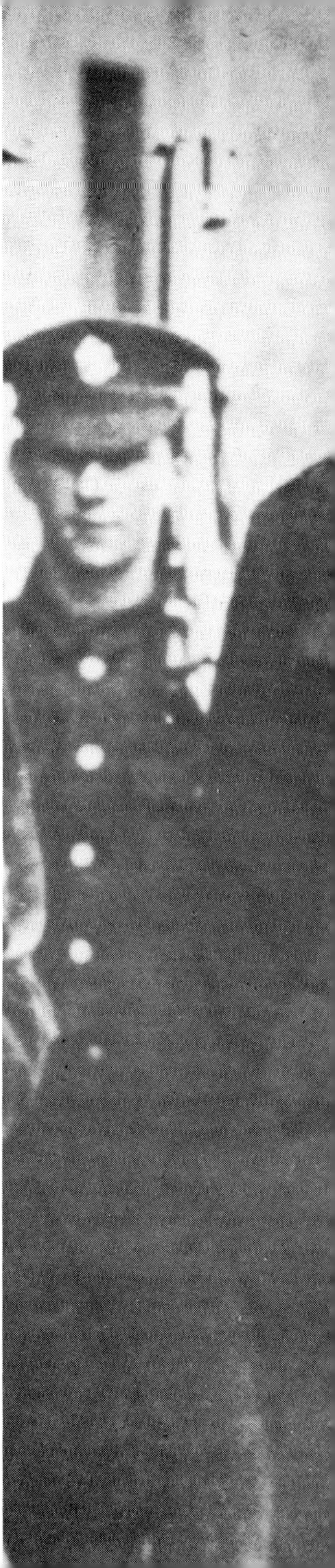

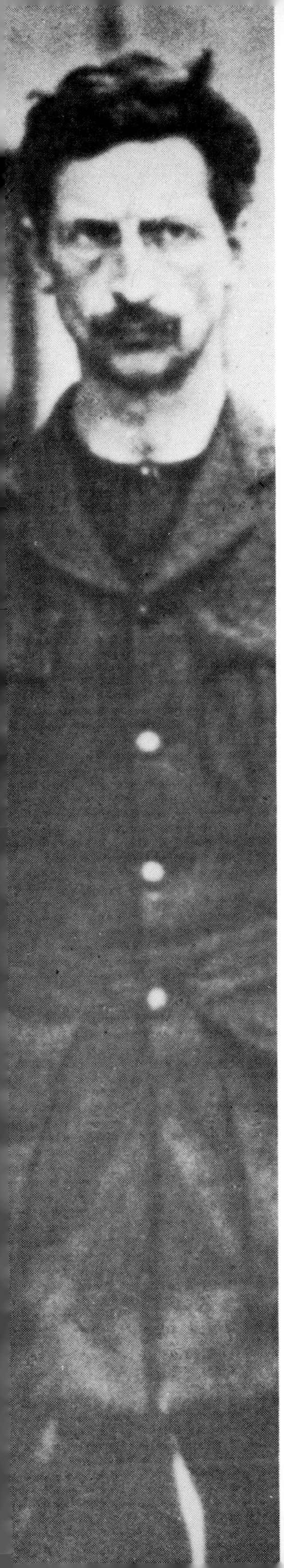

flavour both within the court and without. The death sentence, passed according to this usually obsolete and almost incomprehensible bill, seemed to many to be a mere act of political vengeance by Smith, representing the British government, on Casement, representing Irish opposition to the government in his own country. A great many people, in England, Ireland, and the United States, felt that Casement should not be hanged. In order to deal with this measure of opposition, British intelligence therefore circulated some so-called diaries of Casement's – almost certainly forged – according to which he was not only a homosexual (he may have been) but engaged in particularly disgusting sexual practices. As was realised by those who ordered the forgeries, the mere existence of these documents made it extremely difficult for the leaders of opinion in Britain and the United States to defend Casement in 1916. (This technique of using forged documents had been employed against Parnell by *The Times* with the Piggott letter of 1887, and was to be used again by the Conservative Party with the Zinoviev letter of 1924. Political intelligence staffs and semi-official journalists run true to form.)

Asquith soon enough realised that he had made a mistake in his handling of Ireland after the Rising. He tried to pass the blame on to that dull soldier, General Maxwell, and fired him. It was too late, both for Ireland and for Asquith. Asquith was supplanted by Lloyd George, and Asquith's gentle and generous Redmondite friends in Ireland were replaced by *Sinn Fein.* The Rising and the reprisals had made the Revolution inevitable. Sean O'Faolain, that fine writer, has written of his country: 'Most of our physical embodiments of the past are ruins, as most of our songs are songs of defiance.' The Easter Rising was a complete failure: yet without it the Irish might never have been free of English rule. The leaders, alive, had very few supporters even among the Irish patriots: dead they became and have remained their country's heroes. The Easter Rising was a total failure. It was a total success. After Easter Week 1916, permanent English rule in Ireland was an impossibility. This tragedy was a triumph. Other tragedies, and few triumphs, were to follow. But the Irish achieved it, and alone.

Top left: *Padraic Pearse surrendering to Brigadier-General Lowe. As C-in-C of the Irish Republican Forces he regarded it as his duty to surrender before the other commandants.* ***Bottom left:*** *Michael Mallin and the Countess Markievicz, both of the Citizen Army, who had commanded the St Stephens Green strongpoint, after their surrender.* ***Left:*** *Commandant, now President, de Valera, after the surrender of Boland's Mill*

Chapter 6

'Wanton and cruel oppression'

Throughout the remainder of 1916 Ireland lay in a stunned condition. Sixteen of the leaders in the Rising, including Casement, were executed. The most prominent to escape this fate was Eamonn de Valera, who had been born in the United States and could therefore claim American citizenship, though he never in fact did so: he was condemned to penal servitude for life. So too was the Countess Markievicz. But the round-up of suspects went far beyond the actual participants in the Rising. Even Eoin MacNeill received a life sentence. There were some 3,500 arrests, and though 1,000 of these were soon discharged, 2,500—including eighty women—were transferred to English prisons. This is approximately double the number of men who had actually risen in Easter Week. The Republican movement was effectively, if only temporarily, decapitated.

It was while being marched to the ships that were to carry them to their English prisons that the Irishmen first began to sense that maybe all had not been in vain after all. The crowds that had booed them on the day of surrender now cheered and blessed them and women broke through the police cordons to thrust little presents into their hands. They must then have realised that they, and above all their dead leaders, had lit such a candle in Ireland as would not quickly be put out. Even Princes of the Church now spoke up for the rebels, though not for rebellion. Dr O'Dwyer, the Bishop of Limerick, in a published letter to General Maxwell, described the repressive measures as 'wantonly cruel and oppressive'.

American reaction was equally strong or stronger, and extended far beyond the immediate circle of *Clan na Gael,* the extremist Irish-American organisation controlled by the IRB. An Irish Relief Fund was opened, with no less than forty archbishops and bishops among its **90** ▷

Left: *The prisoners were held for some time in Dublin prisons and barracks before the majority were transferred to England and to the Frongoch internment camp in Wales. As this Jack Yeats picture* ***(next page)*** *shows, communicating with the prisoners, as in this case in Sligo jail, was not impossible*

SALA

patrons. Before the end of the year this organisation had collected close on $150,000 (£31,200) for those who had suffered in the Rising—especially the families of the dead and of the imprisoned. This American reaction, even more than the reactions of the indigenous Irish, caused the British government to reconsider its policy. With the failure of the Somme offensive, the stalemate at Verdun, and the defeat of Brusilov's offensive on the Eastern Front, it was becoming increasingly improbable that the Allies could defeat the Central Powers without substantial American support. American goodwill has seldom been of greater importance to Britain. However, no American politician was inclined wantonly to alienate the Irish-American vote—far more homogeneous in those days than it is to-day—by supporting, even tacitly, British repression in Ireland, particularly as this was an election year. President Wilson, running for a second term of office, was already making the principles of national sovereignty and of the right to self-determination of all small nations one of the principal planks in his election platform and, by extension, of American foreign policy.

It was not until early December 1916 that Lloyd George replaced Asquith as leader of the Coalition Government in Britain. He was determined to embroil America in the war, at all costs and by every means. One of his first acts as prime minister was to order the immediate release of all Irish prisoners being held, without trial, in British prisons and concentration camps. They were welcomed as heroes when they landed in Ireland at Christmas time.

Lloyd George had of course been intimately concerned in Irish affairs before ever he became premier. During the summer he had had discussions with Carson and the other Unionist leaders, and had agreed that partition, as tentatively outlined in 1914, must be a basic and permanent element in any Irish political settlement, though what precisely the borders of 'Ulster' were to be was left vague. Redmond, now a spent force, agreed in rather ambiguous terms to this proposed solution. Its very vagueness had immediate and unfortunate results in the north-east. The Protestant mob, chanting its foolish slogan that Home Rule meant Rome Rule, and quite unrestrained by the authorities, increased its attacks upon the Roman Catholic minority, with the avowed intention of driving them from their homes. In the north-east the Irish nationalists were distressed and embittered at the prospect of being forced out or left at the permanent mercy of these savage persecutors. So were many Irishmen in the rest of the country when they contemplated the prospect of partition.

Lloyd George now planned to call a convention of Irish-

men, whose job was to frame proposals for the future government of Ireland, less the Protestant north-east, within the British Empire and swearing allegiance to the King. It was thus with the dual intention of securing peace in Ireland and regaining lost American goodwill that the prisoners were released. Whether or not Lloyd George ever believed that his convention could offer an acceptable solution is neither here nor there: that astute politician needed time, time above all for America to enter the war, and this the unwieldy convention gave him. *Sinn Fein* had boycotted it, and so had important Ulster Unionists. When at last it was wound up, it seems he never bothered to read its final report. By then he had no need to do so.

The new men come forward

It was to a rapidly-changing Ireland that the prisoners returned. *Sinn Fein* had become the dominant, and was soon to be the only, Irish native political force, an almost nationwide opposition to the forces of the Crown. And *Sinn Fein* itself was changing. The party that Arthur Griffith had made some ten years ago, with the intention of creating a Dual Monarchy by methods of passive resistance and political abstention, was becoming the political arm of revolutionary republicanism under the dominance of the newly-recreated Irish Republican Brotherhood. And that organisation, too, was changing. The men who had led the Rising, and in so many cases lost their lives, had been fanatical patriots, perhaps, but they had tended to be theoreticians, dreamers of dreams, amateur poets, men closer in their generation to a Rilke rather than to a Trotsky. The men who took the places of the dead were of a different stuff.

Among those who came back to Dublin from prison for Christmas Day 1916 was Michael Collins. He had fought, as a captain, in the General Post Office, and had later acquired a considerable degree of authority among his fellow-captives in the concentration camp at Frongoch. He was among those who there reorganised the smashed, partly demoralised, and almost leaderless IRB in which he rapidly achieved great, and soon dominant, importance.

Michael Collins was born of poor but not uneducated parents in West Cork, in 1890. He attended the village school and at sixteen went to London to find work, first in the post office, then as an accountant in a banking trust. He read, went to the theatre as often as he could afford, and became a determined Irish patriot. 'The Big

Left: *Prisoners in the yard of Stafford Gaol, one of the English prisons to which men of the Republican movement were sent after the Rising. Most were to be released in December 1916*

Fellow'—the nickname was first one of mockery for his horse-playing, boyish nature, later one of admiration for his very big talents—returned to Ireland early in 1916, after ten years' exile, with a group of Irish friends. They came back in order to avoid British conscription but, more important, to take part in the rebellion which they believed imminent. Collins joined the Volunteers, and in the somewhat chaotic conditions inside the Post Office showed himself to be not only a very brave man but also a good officer. In prison and the concentration camp he established the fact that he was a natural leader.

Essentially self-educated, this very tough soldier was above all an administrator of genius. Though he was, throughout most of his short life, a devout Roman Catholic, he had little time for the respectable, puritanical, lace-curtain Irish priesthood. He liked to drink, to kiss the pretty girls, and he liked to fight. He was a truly heroic Irishman of his age—no other nation could have bred quite such a man, nor perhaps at any other age could Ireland—and this at a time which W.B.Yeats, equally Irish though of another sort, has described brutally as one of 'weasels fighting in a hole'. Collins was also, and undoubtedly, one of the two most important men in the events to come.

De Valera returns

The other was Eamonn de Valera, who was a convict in Maidstone gaol until 16th June 1917. He and the other Republican soldiers were moved to Pentonville prison that day, and on the 17th set free. As he walked out of the prison he was handed a telegram informing him that he had been chosen as a candidate in the by-election for East Clare, on the *Sinn Fein* ticket. He was given a hero's welcome when he landed in Dublin the next day. He and the other released men marched ashore as soldiers. There were bonfires on the hills all over Ireland and torchlight processions and, in Dublin, guards of honour and troop inspections. This was a military event, not a return of felons to their native land. It did not augur well for Lloyd George's convention, just about to begin.

By the time de Valera returned Michael Collins was already on the Supreme Council of the IRB—a society of which de Valera was a member, though he never attended a meeting—and was exercising great influence within the leadership of the Volunteers. He was also secretary of the National Aid Association, with considerable funds from the American Relief Fund and elsewhere. He was thus in direct contact both with individuals and organisations representing the entire Republican movement. He was, in fact, already in a key position as the new phase in Anglo-Irish relations opened.

But now the partners in the *danse macabre* had got out of step. Throughout 1917 the British were anxious to appease Irish wishes, within the framework of partition and allegiance, whereas the Irish were hardening in their demands. *Sinn Fein* was winning elections against the moribund Nationalist Party. Those elected did not take their seats in the United Kingdom Parliament at Westminster, but regarded themselves as the nucleus for a future Irish parliament, *Dail Eireann.* With remarkable speed *Sinn Fein,* which at this moment of history can be more and more identified with the newly-recreated IRB, set about establishing a complete alternative government. More and more, throughout the next two years, the Irish boycotted the British courts of law and used those set up by the Republicans; the Irish Republican Army was being rebuilt, this time with a proper staff apparatus; and, perhaps most important of all, Collins was expanding his National Aid organisation, which had always used its funds for purposes other than those of charity, to be the embryonic exchequer for the still unborn Irish Republic. The rebels of 1916 were becoming the revolutionaries of 1919, and this was a new development in 20th-century Irish history and—with the exception of the ill-digested Boer Republic—in the history of the modern British Empire.

In October 1917 de Valera was elected president of *Sinn Fein,* in succession to Arthur Griffith, and with his election the whole nature of the organisation was changed openly as it had already been altered covertly. It is hard, even now, to describe de Valera either as man or politician. Rigid yet devious, hard yet immensely kind, charming and at times witty in private yet often tactless and on occasion boorish in public, should this not very well-read and prosy mathematician be called narrow-minded and open-hearted or open-minded and narrow-hearted? It is too early to judge, and furthermore he was to change with the years, with responsibility and, perhaps, with regrets that he has never uttered. What does appear is that he belonged, above all the Irish leaders of that generation, to a pattern of public men which was to become very familiar all over Europe within a very few years: he was an ideologue, and to such people words and formulae can mean more than men or even than ideas. Cold, dignified, sensible, and yet inflexible, this great patriot was a strange leader of insurrection. An intensely devout Christian and a most respectable man in his

Left: *Prisoners returning from England, some of them still in their prison uniforms, are fêted through the streets of Dublin. They returned to a rapidly-changing Ireland in which Sinn Fein became the dominant party in total opposition to the Crown*

private life, he had proved his military valour publicly at Boland's Mill, nor did he ever feel the need to do so as a soldier again. At the age of thirty-six, in 1917, he was already a symbolic figure – the only memorable survivor – and this symbolism he was prepared to accept, and to use for his own purposes and for those of his country, for the next half a century and more. Many were to imitate him in this: none to excel. This chilly, charming man of few, passionately held ideals, of fewer ideas and enthusiasms, was at least as 'typical' an Irishman as was Yeats or Collins. Yet Collins and he were almost bound to collide eventually in the situation that was created by the failure of the convention and the resurgence of Irish nationalism.

At first they were close allies. In July 1917 the convention met, and took nearly a year to die a natural death. During the rest of 1917 Ireland was rapidly recovering from the shock of the Rising and the reprisals. De Valera became titular head of the Irish Republican Army as well as president of *Sinn Fein*. He was thus, to all intents, president of a country which did not as yet legally exist, of what certain Frenchmen have described, in their own country's story, the *pays réel* as opposed to the *pays légal*. And an increasingly large proportion of that country's population was preparing to fight, with all the means at its disposal, to make the reality legal too, to fight with the ballot box, with boycott, with guns, and, when imprisoned, with the weapon of the hunger strike. When Thomas Ashe died in Mountjoy Prison in September 1917, the victim of forcible feeding, the people gave him the equivalent of a state funeral. Some 30,000 mourners, led by a company of armed Volunteers, followed his coffin. It seemed that a new eruption could not be long delayed. Yet the Irish leaders wished for delay, since they relied more and more on the eventual peace conference, and American support as promised, to give Ireland her freedom. The clever men of the IRB realised, in early 1918, that American intervention had made the outcome of the war certain. They therefore did their best to restrain their followers from precipitate action, though not always with success. There were riots and skirmishes, with casualties, and inside the prisons the silent struggle went on. The alternative government, which was to take over without bloodshed, was made ready. There were no Irish plans for a rising or a revolution in 1918, or at least none acceptable to the IRB.

In early 1918 the attitude of the British government now veered about once again, and most violently. Just as the Irish were now looking forward to a postwar settlement on the lines of Wilson's Fourteen Points, so the British dreaded a peace settlement involving Irish

affairs that must be dominated by United States power. For the time being, however, the United States were fully committed to the war against the Central Powers and were thus unlikely to give any sort of support to an Irish rebellion against America's most powerful ally. For all these reasons this was precisely the time when Lloyd George and his Unionist friends in London and Belfast may well have wished to see the Irish rise again, so that the country could be reconquered and silenced without worrying about American opinion too much, and the embryonic government of Ireland destroyed, at least for a generation and with luck forever. Needless to say the provocation that followed was not openly admitted by the British at the time, nor ever has been. It would seem unlikely that such a crime was ever discussed in the Cabinet, nor would this have been necessary.

Conscription is imposed

The one act of administration that was most likely to bring about an Irish insurrection was the enforcement of the Conscription Act. The day he heard that his convention had filed its report, Lloyd George announced that conscription would be imposed throughout Ireland. The one man who represented all that Ireland most disliked about her rulers, Lord French, was appointed Viceroy and Lord Lieutenant in place of the friendly, if ineffectual, Wimborne. His orders were that if there were to be an insurrection, the Irish must fire first. This was, in fact, a political declaration of war. Only Lord French was too stupid to do his job properly (indeed it was many years since this man had done any job properly) and the Irish leaders were too clever to fall into so obvious a trap. There were continuing skirmishes, with a few casualties, but no revolution, as yet. The Irish were waiting for the peace conference. They were waiting for the Americans, as they had in past centuries waited for the Spaniards and the French, as they had in this waited for the Germans. But *Sinn Fein* was strong, and the Irish leaders were having a difficult time persuading them to wait much longer.

In order that the planned insurrection, planned by the British this time and not by the Irish, should be doomed to complete failure it was also decided by the British authorities that its potential leaders be rounded up, for they wished this to be a *jacquerie,* an inchoate peasants' uprising, a repetition of 1798. Therefore in May of 1918 the British carried out selected arrests. About one hundred men and women were seized and taken to prisons

Left: *Count Plunkett, father of one of the executed leaders, addressing a meeting in 1917 when most prisoners came home*

US
JOHN BULL
FRANCE
HARRY GRANT DART

in England. It is the same familiar list of names: Griffith, Cosgrave, de Valera, Markievicz, the widows of Sean MacBride and of Thomas Clarke. The leadership of *Sinn Fein* and of the Volunteers was once more in the bag. Michael Collins was one of the very few to escape the net. With a price on his head, which eventually reached £10,000, he remained very much at large, in Ireland, on the run for some three years, and during that time virtually in charge not only of the Irish revolutionary forces but also, and in a way paradoxically, of the Irish Republican Government.

Speaking for, and increasingly as, the IRB he managed to prevent the Irish revolution which the British wanted in wartime, until after that war was over. At the same time he most brilliantly organised a large, publicly subscribed Irish Republican bond issue. A difficult operation at the best of times, almost impossible when files have to be hidden or removed at the policeman's knock, by day or night, in a matter of seconds. All this was for the future government. For the coming revolution, if it must come, he set about penetrating the British intelligence apparatus in Ireland and creating a counter-intelligence of his own. Without the preparations that Collins and others made in 1918, the Anglo-Irish War of the following year would undoubtedly have been the *jacquerie* and consequent massacre that the Lloyd George government then apparently desired.

By 11th November 1918 the number of Irish Volunteers, commanded by the still imprisoned President de Valera but effectively controlled by the IRB and particularly by Michael Collins, numbered some 100,000 men, most of them unarmed. Some 50,000 Irishmen had lost their lives, fighting for Britain, in the war that finished on that day.

Lloyd George called a snap election, the so-called Khaki Election. *Sinn Fein* contested every seat in Ireland except those for Trinity College, by accident the North Down seat, and four further seats in Ulster which were, by agreement, allotted to Redmond's Parliamentary Party rather than split the anti-Unionist vote. The Irish Labour Party, for similar reasons, put up no candidates. The election thus became something of a plebiscite, for or against a republic.

The result was a landslide. Redmond's party, eighty-four strong in the previous parliament, now held only seven

Top left: *Uncle Sam warns Sinn Fein against stabbing America's new ally in the back. The Republican cause could expect little help from the United States in its struggle against Great Britain until the war was over.* ***Bottom left:*** *De Valera during elections for Dail Eireann, 1918.* ***Left:*** *De Valera in America, 1919* seats, four of them the Ulster seats not contested by *Sinn Fein.* The Unionists held twenty-five, including the four from Trinity College which was then the modern equivalent of a rotten borough. *Sinn Fein* had retained or won the remaining seventy-three. In all Ireland some 70 per cent of those who went to the polls had voted *Sinn Fein,* some 20 per cent Unionist. Thus did the Irish people deny the British propagandists' claim that Irish republicanism represented nothing save a handful of fanatics, now safely locked up in English gaols.

The *Sinn Fein* MPs did not attend the United Kingdom parliament in Westminster. *Dail Eireann* was now convened, to which all members elected by Irish constituencies, regardless of party, were invited. When the first Dail met, on 21st January 1919, it was in fact only the *Sinn Fein* members who attended, and of those thirty-six out of seventy-three were in English prisons. When the roll-call was read, and the names of those thirty-six not answered, the clerks announced, in Irish: 'Imprisoned by the foreign enemy.' But the thirty-seven who were there added a skeleton legislature to the shadow of a judicial system, army, and exchequer already prepared to obey an as yet nonexistent Irish state.

On the day that the first Dail met two members of the Royal Irish Constabulary were shot while escorting a consignment of dynamite, to be used for blasting operations. Their killers were members of the Irish Volunteers, who desired the explosives for other purposes. It is generally agreed that these were the opening shots in the Irish Revolution.

In February 1919 Michael Collins and Harry Boland went to England and themselves sprang de Valera from Lincoln Prison, together with a couple of other Irishmen held there. Dublin wished to give de Valera the sort of reception to which he was becoming accustomed, but on an even larger scale. And, since the British Home Office had covered their mortification at his release by announcing that it was the Home Office which had released him, there seems little reason why there should not have been fireworks over the Liffey such as, in years past, had welcomed a King or Queen of England. De Valera refused these honours. He foresaw that there might be violence, with strong British reactions, and he, like the other Irish leaders, was still relying on the Paris peace conference to give Ireland her freedom without further bloodshed. In March 1919 the British released their other Irish prisoners. In Ireland, both in the north-east and in the rest of the island, unrest and violence increased.

In April 1919 de Valera presided over an open meeting of the first Dail, of which he had been elected president. Sean T. O'Kelly was in Paris, attempting, and failing, to

have the Irish Republican case presented at the peace conference.

By June it had become apparent that Irish aspirations were not to be given a hearing by the Allied delegates at the Versailles Conference. That same month de Valera left for America to secure support for an Irish revolution that was now and inevitably imminent.

He was to be in America for over a year, and was to prove himself perhaps the most superb propagandist that even this century of great political propaganda has yet seen. With him away, Michael Collins remained the effective leader of a revolution that was now both inevitable, immediate, and prepared against on both sides. The Americans had joined those other foreign friends, Spanish, French, and German, on whom the Irish could not rely. The Irish therefore had once again no choice, if they were to act at all. They must do it, as best or worst they could, on their own. A time of horror settled upon Ireland. And Yeats wrote in that year, long before the full horror was realised:

Violence upon the roads; violence of horses;
Some few have handsome riders, are garlanded
On delicate sensitive ear or tossing mane,
But wearied running round and round in their courses
All break and vanish, and evil gathers head. . . .

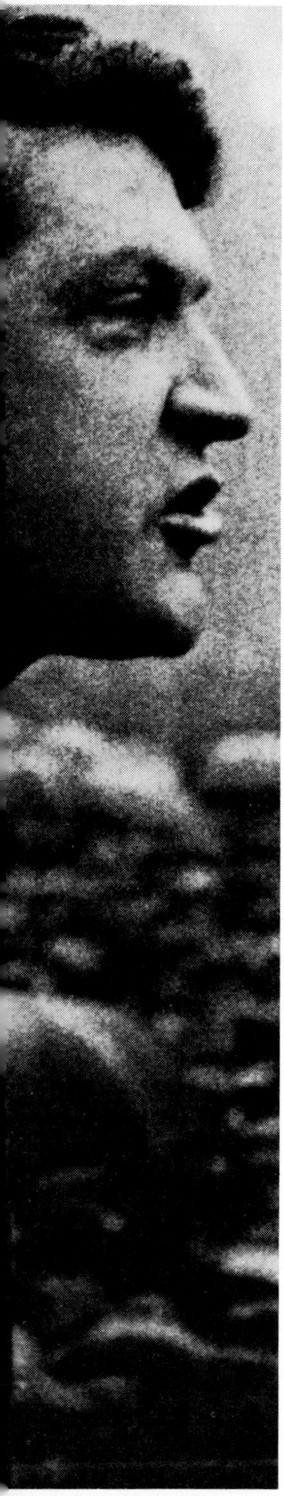

Left: *Michael Collins, one of the two great figures in the latter stages of Ireland's struggle for freedom. Friend and partner of de Valera during the fighting against the British, the two were tragically on opposing sides in the civil war after independence. Collins was to be killed in an ambush—the most prominent of the many leaders of the successful struggle who fell to the bullets of their former comrades-in-arms*

Chapter 7

Freedom and civil war

The Anglo-Irish War assumed the proportions of a war in the summer of 1919, and lasted for some two years. Like all guerrilla wars it was a dirty fight, atrocities breeding atrocities, vengeance following upon revenge. Murder was a weapon of war acceptable to both sides, though on the whole the Irish murdered selectively, the British with less discrimination. Some British units tortured their prisoners; some Irish tortured captured informers. There was much treachery, and little gallantry. The sudden ambush on the mountain lane; the raid in the night and the English officer or Irish leader shot in front of wife and children; the knife between the shoulder-blades in the dark, slum alley-way; the moment of awareness in the public house when the victim suddenly realises that these men are not his friends, that he is alone with them, and that his lower lip is beginning to tremble; the lorry careering down a long village street, its machine-guns blazing blindly into unidentified little homes; drunken soldiers burning half Cork as a reprisal; Michael Collins's squad of professional assassins stalking their victims through the quiet and leafy suburbs; big, beautiful, Georgian country houses blazing in the night, because their owners probably had Unionist sympathies; infuriated soldiers shooting into the massed spectators at a football match; and always the glance over the shoulder, the backward glance of fear. That is guerrilla warfare.

And yet the casualties were astonishingly small. Absolute figures are for obvious reasons unobtainable, but the most reliable estimate is that perhaps some 300 servants of the Crown were killed, perhaps some 800 Irishmen and women, while damage to property has been assessed at a mere £5,500,000 in the currency of the time. When it is remembered that the British army in Ireland alone was some 80,000 strong—quite apart from the constabulary and the various auxiliary forces—the smallness of these casualty figures is surely amazing. When one considers the vast results that have flowed more or less directly from the events then being unfolded in

Left: *A British Auxiliary searches a suspect during the civil war*

MOTORS

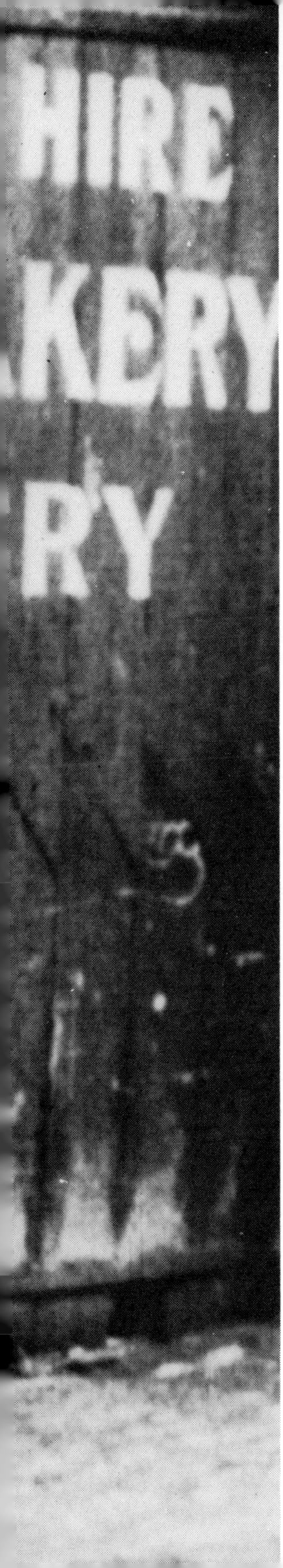

Ireland, the loss of Empire, the eclipse of Britain as a world power, perhaps even the toppling of Western man from his Victorian pinnacle of world power, these small events in a small country on the outermost confines of Europe resemble a mountain spring, high in the Rockies: in due course that bubbling stream will debouch into the Gulf of Mexico as part of the Mississippi river, its parent and its child.

The primary reason for the small number of casualties lay in the nature of the war that the Irish now fought against the English. In a guerrilla war between irregulars and regular forces, it is the guerrillas who set the strategy, and in considerable measure the tactics, to which the regular forces are more or less compelled to respond. Though the British had overwhelming strength, the Irish held the initiative, at least throughout most of the fighting, and called the tune in this phase of the *danse macabre*. It would seem probable that there were never more than 2,000 Irishmen under arms, though in compensation for this vast disparity of force the Irish enjoyed the support of the overwhelming majority of their compatriots. But this disparity meant that the Irish must, so far as possible, avoid any sort of pitched battle with the forces of the Crown, and indeed when such encounters did take place the Irish were usually the losers.

Michael Collins, who among the rebel leaders became more and more effectively in charge, and his small staff, therefore set about implementing *Sinn Fein* policy on a basis other than that of direct confrontation. It was Irish policy to make British rule in Ireland irrelevant and eventually impossible. The military corollary to this policy was to render the forces of the Crown inoperative. And the quickest and maybe easiest way to do this was to blind those forces: to deprive them of their eyes by destroying their intelligence apparatus. Although there were armed clashes, the essential struggle was between Michael Collins's intelligence service and that of Dublin Castle. Collins, who received moral and financial support from de Valera and the Americans, proved himself a genius at this type of operation which indeed he may be said to have invented. The British, once they grasped the true nature of the war, sent in specialist reinforcements from London. Fourteen of these imported intelligence officers, living as civilians, were murdered by Collins's squad on 'Bloody Sunday', 21st November 1920, in their lodgings. This was perhaps Collins's most spectacular and successful coup. It was hardly an act of great chivalry, but by that time much had happened in Ireland.

Left: *Watchful men of the RIC during a house-to-house search*

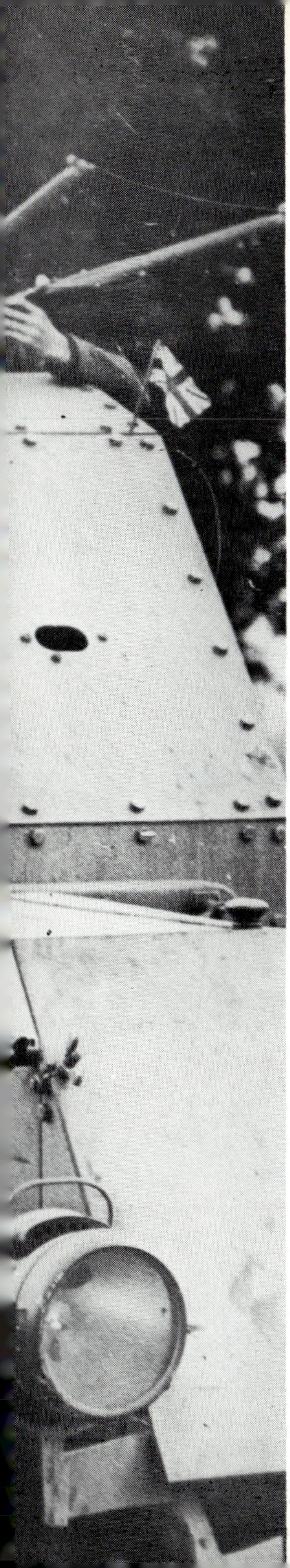

In August 1919 the members of the Dail swore allegiance to the republic, while the men of the Irish Republican Army recognised the members of the Dail, headed by the absent President de Valera, as that republic's provisional government. In those early days clashes between the forces of the Crown and those of the republic were largely motivated by the desires of the Irishmen to obtain arms, particularly from the Royal Irish Constabulary. Rapidly these scattered and uncoordinated operations became a systematic attack upon the RIC as such, first in the west and south, then in the rest of Ireland with the exception of most of the north-east. If 1916 had been essentially urban, indeed almost entirely limited to Dublin, 1919-21 was predominantly rural. In the countryside the RIC was the most effective force in the service of the Crown. The British army was better armed and better equipped but lacked the RIC's intimate knowledge both of persons and of places. Therefore, as a major operation in his intelligence war, Collins was determined first to isolate the men of the RIC within their own districts and then to eliminate the force as a whole.

This was not kept secret from the constables, who were urged by arguments of varying sorts to resign from the force. In increasing numbers they did so, some because their sympathies lay with their compatriots of the Republican Army, others because life in the RIC was becoming just too dangerous. By August of 1920 about a thousand men had resigned, or some 10 per cent of the force, while recruiting in Ireland had ceased completely. Those who remained were compelled more and more to retreat into the comparative safety of their fortified barracks, where they lived a life of siege punctuated by an occasional sally on the part of the RIC, an occasional assault on the part of the Republicans. Being thus cut off from the normal life of the districts in which they served, they had ceased to provide Dublin Castle with the basic intelligence it required. Indeed save in so far as they acted as scouts for the military and for the irregulars arriving from England, they were no longer a power in the land. Outside almost every town and many an Irish village there is a comparatively modern ruin, the barracks of the RIC. These are perhaps the most tangible battle trophies to Collins and his flying columns.

In Dublin, Collins set about penetrating the British administrative apparatus at the highest level. At least two senior detectives in the Special Branch were working for him, and on one occasion he personally inspected the files of that political and counter-espionage branch of the police. His own near-miraculous escapes—he walked 110 ▷

Left: *The British troops relied heavily on armoured cars*

'Evil gathers head'

It was warfare once again, and once again the British destroyed property in their attempt to crush the Irish. If the burning of Cork was the most spectacular example of this, the villages also were not spared **(below)**. The forces of the Crown, reinforced by their irregular helpers **(right),** increasingly engaged in wholesale reprisals against the civilian population, at first unofficially, later officially. In return the Irish destroyed the British administrative centres. However, stalemate was reached and on 4th July 1921, to the joy of the Irish **(next page),** a truce was agreed and eventually a treaty was signed by the Irish **(next page top)** and the British, to the relief not only of Lloyd George and F.E.Smith but also of King George V **(next page centre)** who intervened personally to secure peace. The new Irish parliament met under heavy guard **(next page bottom)** but there were many Irishmen, including de Valera, who believed that their delegation had given away too much to the British

and rode about Dublin with no attempt at disguise – can in some measure be ascribed to the tips he received from these friends on the other side, in some to the certain fate that must await the informer who denounced the Big Fellow. Yet to this writer, at least, it seems almost incredible that the British failed to pick him up. Did they, perhaps, not really wish to do so? Had some clever man in Whitehall realised that eventually there must be negotiations, that the pragmatist Collins would be a more tractable negotiator than the ideologue de Valera, and that there was no third Irish figure of comparable stature on the scene? This is pure speculation, for which there is no evidence whatsoever.

The Irish Republic's own intelligence network was broadly based. Throughout the Irish countryside, and even in the cities, it knew pretty well everything that was going on. It went further. Having himself worked in the London post office, Collins knew how many postal employees were Irishmen and therefore actual or potential allies. Using their services, his intelligence staff was soon reading a high proportion of the British administration's and army's official mail as well as tapping many telephones in Dublin and in London. Irish clerks worked in other branches of the British administration, including the War Office itself. There were many Irish seamen working aboard British and foreign ships. They provided an invaluable courier service, to America and other lands, and this service could and also did smuggle men and arms into, and men out of, Ireland. The Irish provisional government had its own portable printing press which not only printed its own official newspaper, *The Irish Bulletin,* and proclamations, but also the government bonds being sold in America and elsewhere. An Irish Republican Land Bank was opened, to continue the financing of small farmers purchasing their properties. Meanwhile, in order to confuse the British exchequer yet further, Collins's squad destroyed as many of the files of the Inland Revenue and associate organisations as it could lay its hands on. The administration of British justice in Ireland had been rendered almost impossible by boycott and the mass resignation of magistrates. The collection of taxes now became, for a while, another historical memory. In so far as British government still existed in Ireland at all, as 1920 became 1921, it was military government of the purest form, the government of the battlefield, as martial law was gradually extended across almost the entire country.

British reaction to Irish guerrilla strategy was pre-

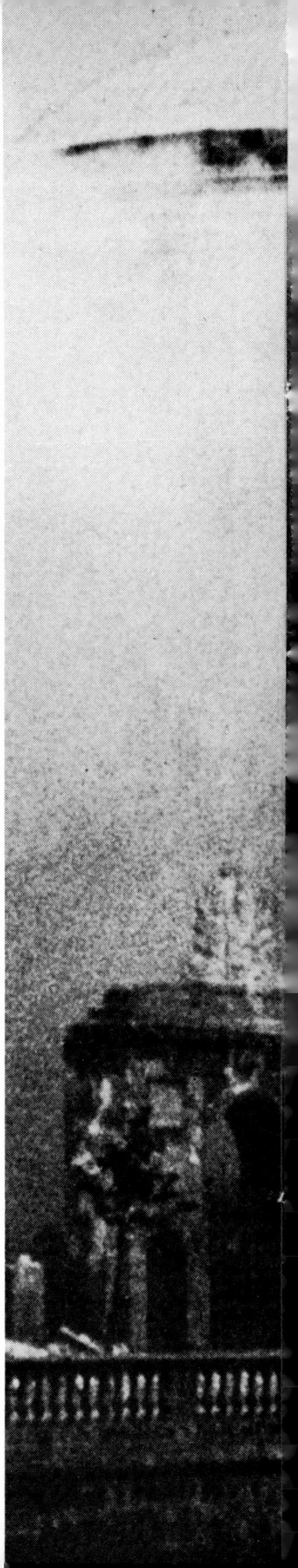

Right: *Anti-treaty forces occupied the Four Courts, the Free State Army shelled it. The Four Courts burned, civil war began*

dictable, clumsy, and ineffective. On the wider stage of world history Britain, by 1920, had little to fear save reproaches from an isolationist America that was about to send Warren Harding to the White House. At home Lloyd George had equally little to fear from his political enemies. Only the British Labour Party, and in general only its cranky, pacifist left wing, expressed sympathy for Ireland, and in 1920 that fraction of the Left was a politically negligible force. Lloyd George was assured of the support of Liberal Unionists and of Conservative Unionists alike in his determination to crush rebellion in Ireland with all the apparently vast and unanswerable means now at his disposal. This was to be the showdown.

The pattern of British reaction was set in Fermoy, County Cork, as early as September 1919. On the 7th of that month Liam Lynch, commandant of Cork Number Two Brigade of the Irish Republican Army, attacked a party of British soldiers, one of whom was killed. The next day, two hundred British soldiers sacked the little market town. Members of *Dail Eireann* protested, and three days later the Dail was declared 'a dangerous association' and prohibited. (Such of its members as were not in prison met henceforth in secret.) Thus the British authorities had, on the one hand, denied any form of legality to their Irish enemies, while simultaneously condoning and indeed encouraging the grossest illegality on the part of their own armed forces. Assassination and reprisals against the civil population became the pattern for the next two years. In the words of that Irish Unionist, General Sir Henry Wilson, then Chief of the Imperial General Staff and soon to be murdered by Irish gunmen on his own front doorstep in London, the British government now believed in 'stamping out rebellion with a strong hand'. In plainer English, this meant a policy of terrorisation: in Ulster by the Protestant mob, in the other three provinces – since neither the RIC nor the British army was ultimately capable of implementing such a policy – by imported auxiliary forces. Recruiting for such a force – the 'Black and Tans' – began in England in the spring of 1920.

The Black and Tans derived their nickname from the hounds of the Limerick hunt which are that colour: they were dressed in uniform, some wearing the black jackets of the RIC over the khaki trousers of the British soldier, others vice versa. This sartorial inelegance was symptomatic of the whole corps which was neither a military force – it was not subject to army discipline – nor a police

Top: *Free State Army using British artillery to bombard the Four Courts.* ***Bottom:*** *Free State officers with an armoured car*

force in any meaningful sense. All over Europe, in 1920, there were young men who had gone straight from school into the trenches and who knew no life save that of soldiers. This pathetic human débris from a most terrible war provided the men who marched on Rome with Mussolini, fought on the German frontiers with the *Freikorps* and later became the nucleus of the Nazi Party, served on both sides in the Russian Civil War. In Britain some of them joined the Black and Tans, created to supplement the dwindling forces of the RIC, while a number of their officers joined a somewhat more formidable force, the Auxiliaries, intended to terrorise more selectively and effectively.

The Black and Tans could not replace the vanishing RIC, nor could the Auxiliaries effectively supplement British military intelligence in Ireland. The Tans seem to have agreed among themselves, erroneously as it turned out, that alcohol was the ideal weapon with which to defeat the Irish, and thereupon set about swallowing as much of the stuff as they could buy, steal, or loot. Here, however, they were up against experts. Many a Black and Tan, unable to distinguish between whiskey and poteen, would wake up – if he woke at all, but they were usually allowed to do so – to find himself far from his base and certainly without his rifle. The Auxiliaries seem to have preferred suavity, charm and a premature James Bond-type toughness. But they, too, were dealing with experts, on the experts' own ground, in the experts' own country. Their chances of survival were smaller than those of their colleagues in the Black and Tans. In retrospect the British auxiliary forces in Ireland during the 'Troubles' seem to have behaved like sad, bad-mannered, and obviously frightened boobies, much as the German irregular forces behaved in their Occupied Territories during the Second World War, much as others have behaved elsewhere before and, alas, since, and predictably will so behave in the future.

This, of course, is not the way that wars are won, nor even colonial rebellions crushed. The British seem to have learned few, if any, lessons from the failure to crush Irish resistance and, indeed, applied the same methods throughout large parts of their revolting empire in the decades to come. The colonial rebels seem to have studied the methods of the Irish with greater care, and often to have copied them, invariably with success. One day an historian will discover how much attention was paid in Asia and Africa to events in Ireland in 1920 and 1921 – and perhaps how little to events in 1922 and 1923.

British rule in Ireland was rendered impossible by the fact that the tiny minority of Irish activists had the passive, on occasion the active, support of most Irishmen and

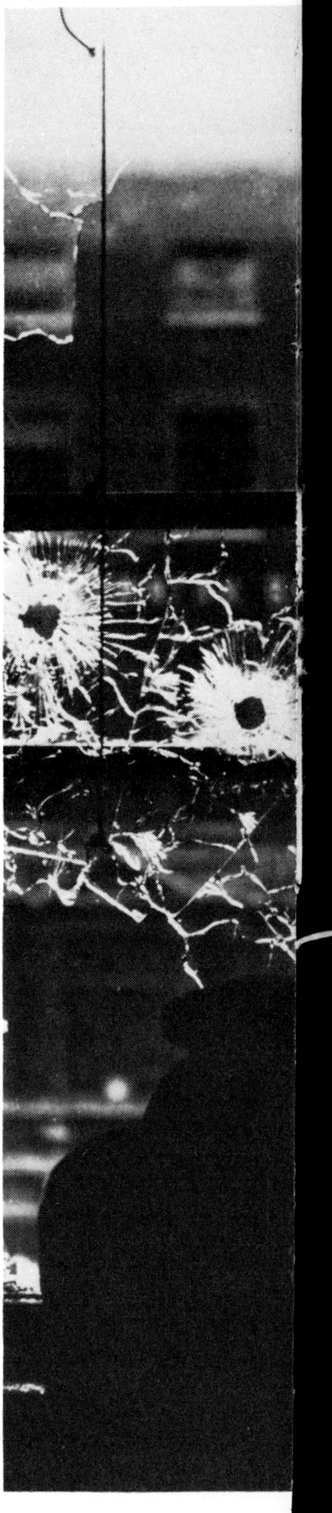

more Irishwomen. British terrorism was extended against the Irish population as a whole. The village creameries, where dairy produce was exchanged and which are an essential mart in a country that relies primarily on cattle, were burned. Cattle markets were forbidden. These clumsy attempts to starve the Irish into submission caused considerable misery but bred contempt for the British and their methods. Yet few Irishmen wished to go on with the fight. It is hardly an exaggeration to say that all Ireland breathed a great sigh of relief when a truce was agreed upon on 11th July 1921, and a few days later an Irish delegation, to be headed as it turned out by Arthur Griffith accompanied by Michael Collins and others, was invited to London to discuss a treaty. This date marks the beginning of the end of British rule in Ireland. According to many it marks the beginning of the dissolution of the still mighty British Empire.

Lloyd George negotiates from strength

It would seem improbable in the extreme that even Lloyd George, let alone his Unionist colleagues, contemplated sabotage of the Empire on so massive a scale. In 1921, when dealing with the Irish, he was acting the British patriot and no doubt believed that he was negotiating from a position of great strength. His Government of Ireland Act had come into force in May: despite the promises of earlier British governments, in all of which he had held high office, to give Ireland Home Rule, Ireland was now partitioned, the first Parliament of Northern Ireland had been elected, and it had met on 7th June 1921. In the eyes of the British and Belfast politicians, and of their legal advisers, partition was thus a *fait accompli* and not a subject meet for discussion at any Anglo-Irish conference.

Furthermore there was evidence of some measure of division among the Irish leaders. De Valera had returned from America in the previous December and it was he, as President of Ireland, who had tentatively accepted Lloyd George's invitation to peace talks. He refused, however, to accept the draft treaty submitted to the Republican Cabinet by the British. He also refused to commit either himself or his high, if still anomalous, office, by personally taking part in the London negotiations concerning the future treaty. De Valera seems at this time to have cast himself, at rather a young age, in the role of 'elder statesman', qualified to adjudicate between the more extremist Republican leaders – principally Collins and the soldiers – and the moderates, such as Griffith, who desired peace at almost any price. That, at least, is how Collins apparently saw the situation when he set off for London early in

Left: *A Free State soldier stands before a shattered window*

October: he certainly did not regard de Valera as more extremist in his republicanism than himself, the leader of the revolution and of the IRB. His delegation had the full status of plenipotentiaries, authorised to agree and sign any document without prior consultation with Dublin, de Valera, *Dail Eireann, Sinn Fein,* or indeed any other branch of Irish government or Irish public opinion.

This, of course, suited Lloyd George. On the British side of the conference table he sat with Winston Churchill, Austen Chamberlain, and Lord Birkenhead (F. E. Smith). Seldom if ever have the British fielded a more formidable team. The Irish delegates were Griffith, Collins, and Barton (who had only recently left prison and was out of touch with activities), supported by two lawyers. Lloyd George can have had little doubt that he and his colleagues could browbeat and hoodwink the Irishmen, all the more so since the Irish Republican Army was near the end of its resources and the Irish people were longing for an end to the horror. That was why he wished the Irish to be plenipotentiaries.

De Valera, on the other hand, took another view in Dublin. He, with Cathal Brugha and Austin Stack, believed that while the Irishmen had full power to negotiate, ratification could only come from *Dail Eireann* which would be advised by the Republican government that de Valera headed.

The conference opened on 11th October 1921, and lasted for two months, in an atmosphere of ever increasing strain, confusion, and what can, at the end, only be described as duplicity. Before the conference began, Irish political prisoners had been released from British gaols, the guns in Ireland fell silent, and over there it was believed, with relief, that the 'Troubles' were over. Michael Collins and the other delegates realised, as the negotiations dragged on, that it would be extremely difficult to recreate, among the Irish population, the will to resist British demands which had existed, in the end reluctantly, before the truce. Furthermore, the Irish delegates soon discovered that they had been summoned to London not to negotiate but merely to sign, to accept less acceptable terms than those offered in the Home Rule Bill of a decade before. Partition, an oath of allegiance to the King, unsatisfactory financial and fiscal arrangements, Lloyd George demanded that they swallow the lot. Some of the Irish delegates seem to have swallowed a great deal of wine and to have enjoyed their trip to London in other ways. Yet when it was serious business, and they hesitated to sign the British government's treaty, Lloyd George began to threaten them with a renewal of the war. This threat at last took the form of an ultimatum, with a twenty-four hour limit. The Irish discussed this at great and bitter

length among themselves. They did not refer the decision to Dublin, but then they were not obliged to do so. They signed, and Collins had the courage to take full personal responsibility for a decision which must have been extremely distasteful to him personally, but which he regarded as essential for the well-being of his country. The whole delegation signed, and with heavy hearts returned to Dublin. De Valera and many others refused to accept the treaty, *Sinn Fein* and the country were split, and within a year Ireland had slid into civil war. Griffith was soon dead, of overwork and maybe a broken heart.

The tragedy of the civil war

An Irish nation had been born at last, but this was not the nation of which Tone and Emmet, Parnell and the Fenians, Pearse and Connolly, even de Valera and Collins had dreamed. Truncated of six of its counties, bitterly divided within itself and impoverished, brutalised by past barbarities and worse to come, a land where the raincoated informer seemed almost Siamese twin to the raincoated gunman, many English Unionists watched with unconcealed delight while Irish shot down Irish and the heroes of last year were ambushed and butchered by the very men whom they had led to a weird and unfulfilled victory that had turned to ashes.

It is not intended here to go into the details of the civil war. The pro-treaty forces, which had become a Free State government with a Free State army, gradually defeated the anti-treaty forces led—though more in theory than in practice—by de Valera. Those forces enjoyed the general support of the militant socialists. The Free State government was backed by the property-owning classes and by the Church. But these divisions were vague and shifting. There was much brutality and treachery in this sickening civil war. It was perhaps inevitable: certainly the blame for its incidence cannot be ascribed to any one man among the Irish leaders, nor collectively to them all. The Free State army, led by Michael Collins until his body lay in his own blood in a back lane near his birthplace, behind Clonakilty in County Cork, and later by General Richard Mulcahy, had the somewhat distasteful support of the British. They triumphed, though that is hardly the word for the peace of the graveyard that descended at last upon Ireland. The Irish Revolution, like so many before and since, had devoured its children. By May 1923 most of the leaders were dead: in the preceding six months the Free State government had executed seventy-seven Republican Volunteers, seventy-seven patriots who had escaped the firing squads of the British. The casualties of

Left: *A heavily-armed but uniformless Free State sentry*

the civil war exceeded greatly those of the Anglo-Irish war.

Some will undoubtedly have taken exception to the word 'revolution' being applied to events in Ireland between 1918 and 1922. The classic revolutions of the past two hundred years have been those in France in 1789, the smothered European revolutions of 1848, the Russian revolution of 1917, and the Chinese revolution of the late 1940's. It has come to be accepted that these great events were in essence and in origin a class struggle with an economic base. This, however, is an over-simplification. That there was a redistribution of wealth, which is not only a symbol of power but also its manifestation and means of exercise, both in France and in Russia, goes without saying. In Ireland there was a redistribution of power as the result of the events here briefly chronicled. The old governing élite was not swept away, nor were its members massacred – an accepted concomitant of 'classic' revolution – yet its power was taken from it. The families who, in 1918, had governed Ireland from London, Dublin, and, to a lesser extent, from their estates and counting-houses for some two hundred and more years found, after all, that they had no natural right to their past eminence. Their main support had been British power, social, economic, political, and ultimately military.

Military power went first. Though Griffith and Collins 'lost' the treaty negotiations, their ultimate victory was assured and the British army had finally left Ireland. Political power moved rapidly into new hands. And though the British still exercise a considerable measure of economic power in the Irish Republic, this form of power is never a fully effective lever without those others. Socially British influence remains considerable but is hardly dominant. The old Ascendancy class has scarcely been spoliated – indeed, perhaps, less so in Ireland than in England – but it has become almost irrelevant, has suffered a fate not dissimilar to that of the French aristocracy after 1830. In the 1920s and 1930s new men took over, with an admirable lack of venom, from the old, to create a new governing class, much as has happened less gently in Russia and elsewhere.

In some respects the Irish 'New Class' copied their predecessors. That class in Ireland has had no more desire to abolish financial differentials than have our contemporaries in Russia. And in both countries the second and third generations accept their status much as the old Ascendancy had done. Furthermore the Irish, rather oddly, accepted and retained the greater part of the old British administrative machinery with its vastly over-

Right: *Irishman searches Irishman during the tragic civil war*

inflated civil service using British methods. On the other hand the men of the New Class in Ireland are an entirely different type from those who ran the country fifty years ago, different in background, different in manner, different perhaps in belief and motive. When a society is thus turned upside down, it will seek a renewed stability and in so doing it must look at the past for models to be accepted or rejected unless its leaders be the purest ideologues in the style of Robespierre or Mao, and such leaders seldom last for long. Imitation is easier and to most people more acceptable than innovation. It is in this context, and in this only, that what took place in Ireland can be called a revolution. Yet the fact that the Irish gained control of their country's destiny, even if they have not always or altogether chosen to exercise it to the full, can hardly be given any other name than revolution.

A competent and most unromantic government ruled the twenty-six counties from the days of the civil war until 1932. William Cosgrave enforced national acceptance of the treaty, carried out many important reforms and much vital reconstruction, did not quarrel with the British, and was vindictive in his treatment of his defeated Irish Republican enemies. In 1932, de Valera, surely one of the great survivors of 20th-century history and this time released from an Irish prison, was back in power. He immediately took a far more positive and aggressive line in his dealings with London: the so-called Anglo-Irish tariff war was the result when the Irish used their political independence to protect their economy. This increased Ireland's economic independence from the larger island, but at a cost. Ireland became increasingly an introspective, retrospective, provincial, *petit bourgeois* state, lacking equally in idealism and in imagination, ruled by small businessmen and machine politicians with the moral backing of a priesthood and a bench of bishops that has not invariably shown wisdom nor even charity. The arts decayed in the decades to come, and the young emigrated as fast as ever they could get out of school. Yeats's terrible beauty had been smothered, in its swaddling clothes, by the civil war and the bitterness that it left behind.

There is little to add. Very skilfully de Valera kept Ireland neutral throughout the Second World War, while leaving to Irishmen the proof that they have little sympathy for the sort of tyranny that Hitler wished to impose upon small nations. Paradoxically, and one cannot end this brief chronicle without another note of paradox, it was not de Valera, with his passion for words and formulae, who at last proclaimed an Irish Republic before all the world, in 1949, but his successors of the coalition government.

It made no difference, then, for this was merely the stirring of long-cold ashes. Ireland had already been an independent political state for many years. Only the issue of partition remained. Attempts to solve this by violence on the part of a new IRA in the 1930s and again in the 1950s were a fiasco. Yet aside from Protestant extremists in the north-east the bitterness has drained away from this sad issue. A sensible solution will surely be reached at last. Then at last the time will have come to write, as Robert Emmet wished, his epitaph and that of the other Irish patriots, in the hope that their descendants may enjoy the happiness and prosperity denied to their ancestors for so long.

Left: *The last flames of violence before peace came to Ireland, the Hammam Hotel fiercely burning in the centre of Dublin*

Chronology of Events

1800 The Act of Union
1846 The Famine in Ireland following a year of bad crops
1848 Insurrection in Ireland led by William Smith O'Brien
1867 The Fenian Rising
1870 Irish Land Act gives tenants compensation for eviction
1881 Gladstone's Land Act gives the small farmer fair rent, freedom to sell his right of occupancy, and fixture of tenancy
1882 Lord Frederick Cavendish and Thomas Burke are murdered at Phoenix Park
1886 Gladstone introduces the First Home Rule Bill in the House of Commons; the bill is defeated and the government falls; there is anti-Catholic rioting in Belfast
1893 The Second Home Rule Bill is defeated in Lords
1903 Land Act sponsored by George Wyndham gives tenant farmers government loans to buy their farms
1910 After two general elections, Unionist results make Labour and Irish support essential if Asquith is to carry through reforms limiting the powers of the House of Lords
1911 Redmond and his supporters vote with the government for payment of MPs, thereby alienating some Irish Nationalists and strengthening the Sinn Fein
1912 **11th April:** introduction of the Third Home Rule Bill
28th September: a Solemn League and Covenant is signed at Belfast pledging resistance to Home Rule and refusal to accept it if it is voted
1913 **1st January:** Sir Edward Carson moves in the House of Commons that Ulster be excluded from Home Rule
The Home Rule Bill is passed twice by the Commons, in January and July, and rejected by the Lords both times
October: Protestant Nationalists hold a meeting in County Antrim at which Sir Roger Casement speaks
1914 **26th May:** the Home Rule Bill is passed for a third time by the Commons; it receives royal assent on 18th September but is not to come into force until after the war
1916 **24th–29th April:** the Easter Rebellion, led by Padraic Pearse, takes place and is suppressed by the British; four leaders are executed and 3,500 arrests made. Sir Roger Casement is condemned to death under the 1351 Treason Act
1918 **14th December:** Sinn Fein candidates win a great victory in the elections for the British Parliament
1919 **21st January:** the Sinn Fein MPs decide not to attend Parliament, and organise the Dail Eireann. The British attempt the suppression of the Sinn Fein movement
1920 **15th May:** the Black and Tans are introduced into Ireland to help crush the movement
23rd December: the Government of Ireland Act is passed by the British Parliament setting up separate parliaments for Northern and Southern Ireland and a Council to effect united action in common affairs
1921 **6th December:** Irish representatives sign a treaty with the British government, granting Ireland Dominion status as the Irish Free State, Northern Ireland retaining the right to adhere to the existing arrangement
1922 **7th January:** the Dail approves the treaty
March: de Valera organises a Republican Society to fight the Nationalists in a civil war
December: the Irish Free State is officially proclaimed and the last British troops leave
1923 **April:** Civil war ends with victory of pro-treaty forces

***Top:** A cartoon showing 'policeman' Gladstone arresting 'Violence' (left); Carson presenting Unionist colours (centre); a Nationalist parade (right). **Centre:** A Unionist poster (left); General Paget, C-in-C in Ireland 1914 (middle); British troops amid the ruins of the GPO in 1916 (right). **Bottom:** Casement under arrest (left); Collins (middle); Free State troops (right)*

Index of main people, places, and events

Author's suggestions for Further Reading

The best general history of Ireland known to this writer is still *A History of Ireland* by Professor Edmund Curtis (Methuen & Co., London, first edition, 1936).

The Making of Modern Ireland 1603-1923 by T.C.Beckett (Faber, London, 1966) is perhaps the best one-volume history of the Anglo-Irish relations

The Irish Question 1840-1921 by Nicholas Mansergh (George Allen and Unwin, London, 1965) deals with Ireland's history in a larger framework, both philosophically and from an international viewpoint. It contains a great deal of most interesting, and illuminating, documentation.

The events of 1916 are well presented by Charles Duff, *Six Days to Shake an Empire* (J.M. Dent & Sons, London, 1966) which also contains a very full bibliography.

The Irish Republic by Dorothy Macardle (Farrar, Straus & Giroux, New York, revised edition, 1951) tells the story of these and subsequent developments with extreme thoroughness, though essentially from the point of view of President de Valera and those who agreed with him. Again, a very full bibliography is provided.

Michael Collins and the Making of a New Ireland by Piaras Beaslai (Dublin, Phoenix Publishing Company, 1926) tells much the same story from another point of view.

Peace by Ordeal by Frank Pakenham (Lord Longford), originally published in 1935, was reissued in a revised edition (Geoffrey Chapman, 1962) and is certainly the most thorough study of the Treaty negotiations. This also contains a full bibliography.

Ireland Since the Rising by Patrick Timothy Coogan (Pall Mall Press, London, 1966) covers not only the earlier material but also the later story of the Irish Republic and has the very considerable advantage of being less partisan than many earlier books. Again, the bibliography is full and reliable.

Constantine FitzGibbon was born in 1919, educated principally in Great Britain and on the Continent, and served throughout the war in the British and American armies. At the end of the war he was a major in Military Intelligence and a specialist on the subject of the German General Staff. Since then he has been a writer, and has written half a dozen novels (of which *When the Kissing Had to Stop* is probably the best known), biographies (including *Life of Dylan Thomas*), and history. His book, *The Shirt of Nessus*, was the first about the attempt to kill Hitler in 1944 to appear in English.

JM Roberts, General Editor of the *Macdonald Library of the 20th Century,* is Fellow and Tutor in Modern History at Merton College, Oxford. He is also General Editor of Purnell's *History of the 20th Century* and Joint-Editor of the *English Historical Review,* and author of *Europe 1880-1945* in the Longman's History of Europe. He has been English Editor of the *Larousse Encyclopedia of Modern History,* has reviewed for *The Observer, New Statesman,* and *Spectator,* and given talks on the BBC.

Library of the 20th Century

Publisher: John Selwyn Gummer
Editor: Christopher Falkus
Executive Editor: Jonathan Martin
Editorial Assistant: Jenny Ashby
Designed by: Brian Mayers/ Germano Facetti
Research: Bruce Bernard

Pictures selected from the following sources

Aras an Uachtaráin 72-3
The Bethmann Archive Inc 136 East 57th St New York N.Y. 10022 Plaza 8-0362 109
BPC Library 12 27 34 41 49 51 57 68 74 96
Brown Brothers, New York 96
Central Press 30 34 38
Imperial War Museum 57
Manchester Evening News & Chronicle 114
Mansell Collection 11
George Morrison 4 7 8 14 15 16 18 21 22 24 27 28 37 39 40 42 44 45 46 47 48 49 54 57 58 61 62 66 74 76 79 82 84 90 92 94 98 102 104 106 107 108 111 113 116 119 120
New Ireland Assurance Co 80
Radio Times Hulton Picture Library 11 32 52 100
Roger-Viollet 96
Sligo Museum, Eire 88-9
Topix 71 74 78